jenny agutter:
a working biography

gary wharton

lushington **PUBLISHING**

for my pal, e.j.p

Published in 2009 by
lushington publishing,
cardiff.

typography + page design:
gary wharton
quadmodbook@yahoo.co.uk

Printed + bound by
HSW Print Ltd
Unit 1
Clydach Vale Industrial Park
Tonypandy
Rhondda CT
CF40 2XX
Tel: 01443 441100

contents

jenny on film

East of Sudan (1964) 85 mins

'The part was that of a little Arab girl who got carried about a lot. I was cast because I was light.' Jenny interviewed in The Guardian, 2002.

Jenny is Asua, a young girl of about ten, looking delightfully cherub-like with a spiky, boyish haircut resembling a young Peter Pan. We only ever see her in a red shirt and trousers and she does come across as very cute (initially she is mistakenly seen as a boy too!) Indeed, cast leads Anthony Quayle and Sylvia Sims had previously acted together in Ice Cold in Alex (1958) and the former enhanced his working association with

Jenny by featuring in The Eagle has Landed (1976) & King of the Wind (1990). All concerned breeze through a screenplay with its copy line of 'You live every terror known to man…when you dare to cross…East of Sudan.' Furnished by scriptwriter Jud Kinberg and helmed by director Nathan Juran, the latter had turned to directing in the 1950s. Sylvia Sims is still acting today and is a marvelous actress that has managed to sustain a varied career; from particular favourites of mine such as Alex as well as The Punch and Judy Man (1963) through to a small screen role as Margaret Thatcher. She had such a beautiful face as a young woman and warms the screen with her presence even in a fluffy part as the governess Margaret, here in East of Sudan. Both the rugged Mr.Quayle and sappy young British officer Derek Foulds (who would later find fame in TV's Heartbeat) immediately fall in love with her but you just know that the former will win her affections. Quayle breezes through his role as Richard, the doer in the film, initially fighting against the younger officer Murchison (Foulds) before finally working in unison to get them all to safety. There is much humour in the screenplay thankfully and as long as the viewer expects little East of Sudan fulfills its criteria. It does bear a resemblance to Cary Grant comedy Father Goose (also released in 1964) in its relationship dynamic of the older male and slightly younger female. The African Queen (1954) is also high on the radar too.

East of Sudan is an odd film due to its clumsy insertion of stock footage from The Four Feathers (1938) to supplement off-screen events surrounding the principal cast. In actuality, these moments prove more entertaining and it really is like someone changing channels when the action returns to the Shepperton studio-bound sets.

Not once do the agreeably impressive sequences of that old film look as if they belong within this feature and it proves grating: badly edited and jaggedly inserted the moments prove embarrassing. However the always splendid Quayle, Foulds, Ms.Sims /Agutter do keep the viewer interested.

Foulds found fame in 1960s-set drama series Heartbeat and is a Rada-trained actor with East of Sudan offering an insubstantial early role. His television career would be highlighted by the popular 1980s political series Yes, Minister and Yes, Prime Minister (which featured another Jenny co-star, Nigel Hawthorne).

Shot in glorious Technicolor jarringly inserted footage of animals ranging from lions, giraffes, hippos and rhinos all seemingly co-existing in the same region when not bumping into the squalid cast. The environment provides plenty of perils for them all and even the human form of an Arab slave ship! In one ridiculous moment, the pint-sized Ms.Agutter is confronted by a rhino (inanely stitched together in a frankly embarrassing manner once more) but manages to avoid being crushed before experiencing the misfortune of falling into a river and almost being eaten by a crocodile. Honestly, and all in the space of almost 90, fun-packed minutes. Goodness knows what 1960s cinema audiences would have made of this upon its original theatrical release (it was a second feature). If this studio-set picture was made today

it would be with a nodding, post-modern wink to the audience but the cast here really had to pretend that it was real. They do a good job but the artificial medium (ropey back projection) would let anyone down. It does have a lovely soundtrack though. Watching the VHS release of the film, some establishing moments of the story are strangely missing: a night time attack on British troops and following attack on a village where the 4 main characters are located sees them manage to escape in a boat are absent.

That error aside, it is a rare treat to see a 'little' Jenny featured in East of Sudan after knowing her later work in such projects as The Railway Children or An American Werewolf in London.

Critical comments:

'This film is a riot of history, geography and ethnology - about which the makers seem to know little and care even less. It might have equally been called 'North, South, or West of the Sudan' or even 'Carry On Doctor Livingstone'.
(Ref: Ian Wright, Guardian, 7 August 1964)

'A thrill-a-minute show which should be a safe bet for the family these holidays.'
(Ref: Ernest Betts, People, 9 August 1964)

'The purest hokum.'
(Ref: Leslie Halliwell)

A Man Could Get Killed (1966) 98 mins
'I say, you're American!'
This is very much in the category of frothy 1960s

comedy with an espionage theme of no real depth. An amiable James Garner stars in a film wherein everyone feels the need to explain themselves as the story concludes. A long-time actor, Garner found renewed fame in the 1970s with telly series The Rockford Files after original small-screen success in Maverick, some two decades earlier. Greek star Melina Mercouri, who would make sporadic film appearances, co-stars. All teeth and bulging eyes, she seems to be playing in a screwball Grant/ Hepburn comedy from the 1930s. Whilst Mr.Garner never let's his guard down to enjoy too much of what's frenetically going on around him (except for kissing his co-star often!) His character is mistakenly believed to be a British spy freshly arrived in Lisbon where he is greeted at the airport by a stereotypical 'man from the Ministry'; all bowler hat and umbrella despite the blazing sunshine. It is a shame really, as this was co-written by T.E.B Clarke and Richard L.Breen: Academy Award-winners, both. The screenplay came from the 1966 novel Diamonds for Danger, written by David E.Walker; one of 2 of his books turned into films.

Co-directed by Ronald Neame and Cliff Owen, they use music well to heighten the humour but despite this lightness, there are quite a few murders of fellow spies/ smugglers laughed off during the feature. Neame worked his way up through the industry as a cinematographer/writer/ director and producer which included the likes of Brief Encounter and early Alfred Hitchcock pictures. In a 2006 Radio 4 interview with Francine Stock, she termed him as being 'a man whose had a career that reads like a history of British film.' Whilst his co-director went on to helm a couple of the mildy-amusing Morecambe & Wise film comedies.

Released theatrically in May 1966, what about Jenny's connection to this film? Well, she is listed in the cast as Linda Frazier, daughter of Sir Huntley (a chess-obsessed Cecil Parker) and Lady Frazier but I failed to observe her appearance. It has been stated that she was an extra at the airport scene or in the pre-credits but if anyone can enlighten me as where she can actually be seen I would welcome any comments. Bubbly blond Sandra Dee co-stars.

Bert Kaempfert's soundtrack for the film includes the first appearance of his most famous composition, 'Strangers in the Night,' here still without lyrics and title but clearly recognizable. It won a 1967 Golden Globe award for Best Original Song in a Motion Picture. The score was released commercially on the Decca label.

Critical comments:

'With a great supporting cast...the movie entertains with tons of tongue in cheek, cloak and dagger sexy verve. It's a fun in the sun movie with all the stars putting in great performances.' (REF: mrcaw@aol.com, Imdb.co.uk)

Gates to Paradise (1968) 89 mins

'Destined to be the most controversial film of 1968. A year in production…'
Film poster advertisement

This was the first English-language feature from esteemed Polish director Andrezj Wajda and was 1 of 2 of his films released in 1968. Over the prevailing years of his long career, Wajda (pronounced VY-da) has received 4 Academy Award nominations and an Honorary Oscar for his work. Makings films since the 1950s, he still continues to this day. Jenny's theatre co-star Sir John Gielgud who worked with Wajda, termed him a 'brilliant director' whilst writing in his diaries. Born in Warsaw in 1927, the director worked with Jerzy Andrzejewski on a screenplay that developed into Gates to Paradise after taking its source from the latter's novella 'Bramy Raju.' That story was made up of 2 sentences; one of a hundred or so pages and the other, a single line. It consists of 40,000 words with no punctuation.

Just how Jenny found herself cast as Maud alongside future Hart to Hart telly star Lionel Stander, here in a serious role and recently described by telly co-star Robert Wagner as 'a wonderful actor,' remains a mystery. Released in June of 1968, Gates to Paradise was an international co-production much to the chagrin of the director. 'This production seemed,' he begins on his excellent website, (see bibliography) 'much like its subject, somewhat doomed from the start.'

The premise for the movie focussed upon an ill-fated crusade by French and German children in 1212 to reclaim Jerusalem from the Saracens. As far as I am aware Gates to Paradise has never been released commercially on VHS or DVD but does occasionally appear at international film festivals.
Critical comments:

'The fact is that all of Wajda's films derive their power from the way they have joined in - or even triggered off - some significant debate, historical, ideological, or social. Gates of Paradise, on the other hand, based as it was on a hauntingly written, extremely intelligent but slightly timeless story, was not only a limp piece of filmmaking, but worst of all a completely damp squib as far as striking any contemporary sparks was concerned.' (Ref: B. Michalek, The Cinema of Andrzej Wajda)
'The director has created a vivid series of images for his tragic tale of innocence overthrown, in which truth is the real murderer of idealized hopes.' (Ref: Albert Johnson /ssfc.com)

Star! (1968) 173 mins

'She needs more than a glamorous mum floating in and out of her life like a female Father Christmas.' Known as the 'lost' Julie Andrews musical, Star! re-teamed the massively successful actor-director-producer team behind The Sound of Music (1965) for this big screen, loosely-chronological biography of musical theatre performer Gertrude Lawrence. It offers Ms.Andrews the opportunity to perform with such gusto that it proves to be a great ride for the audience too. Much has been written about its poor box-office performance, subsequent re-editing/ re-cutting fiasco but there is an awful lot to like about Star!

Jenny portrays Pamela, Gertie's young daughter with whom she barely has much of a relationship with due to the theatrical commitments of her mother. Not quite a teenager, Jenny looks demure and shares three brief scenes with Julie: i) playing badminton on the lawn of a plush French holiday home, ii) methodically quizzing her mother about the absence of her father (played by Yorkshire-born actor John Collin) & iii) politely asking mother if she could return to England to rejoin her school friends much to the disguised disappoint-ment of the former.

Interviewed for the comprehensive DVD release from 20th Century Fox Jenny remembers her screen mother as being totally 'non-starry' and that working for her 'charming and straightforward' director Robert Wise, proved an enjoyable experience. As was the on-set involvement overall for the not-quite thirteen year old.

Principal photography commenced in April '67 but unseasonable bad weather meant that Jenny and the cast/ crew spent three weeks in the south of France instead of the expected single week filming schedule. That was hastily re-worked and saw an internal scene being shot first in June of that year prior to decent weather returning. The location shoot took place at Villa La Serena, Cap Ferrat. Star! was a hugely detailed film production and cost a massive $14 million to produce, which by 1960s financial standards was substantial. Some 185 sets were built across 9 huge stages at 20th Century Fox and the studio mounted an all-out PR assault with exclusive previews and saturation point advertising. Alas, it made little difference as the movie failed to find its audience as fans of Ms.Andrews were not keen to see a more adult Julie on-screen. This was compounded by the fact that most Americans in the mid-1960s were unaware of who Gertrude Lawrence was.

Jenny attended the world premiere of Star! at the Dominion theatre, London on July '68 amidst a blitzkrieg of publicity to generate interest in the film. It is still in use as a theatre but no longer hosts film premieres. Its sold out charity gala was enjoyed by a 1400-strong audience and initial press response proved positive. Star! did good business in both Britain and Japan but despite Fox making cuts to its elongated 3-hours+ running time, it still flopped commercially in the all-important American market. A victim of one cut saw a sequence featuring Jenny and Julie on a lawn and a subsequent 2 hour length was put out in October '69 under the re-titled Those were the Happy Times! Despite 7 Academy Award film nominations plus a Writers Guild of America shout for British-born screenwriter William Fairchild it made little impact. Termed as 'A Totally Wonderful

Musical Entertainment' on its UK poster the film eventually found its way on to terrestrial television in December '74 in its virtually un-cut format. Some brief theatrical presentations followed in the early-1980s both here and in the States too. So if you seek it out expecting to see a dire Julie Andrews musical, you may

well be in for a surprise: because, it's really a rather good watch.

Of incidental note, in its cast was an Oscar-nominated Daniel Massey as Gertie's life-long friend and co-performer, Noel Coward. Richard Crenna, later to star alongside an adult Jenny in the mini-series Mayflower: The Pilgrim's Adventure (1979) features late on in the film too. And as mentioned, John Collin plays Gertie's first husband and on-screen father of Pamela (Jenny). A versatile television actor primarily, Mr. Collin was also cast as Jenny's dad in a 1967 television episode of Boy Meets Girl. Coincidentally, the closing song in Star! is called 'Jenny'.

Critical comments:

'Some believe it actually contributed to the decline of the film musical, whilst also damaging Julie Andrews's career.' (Ref: Stephanie Pinter, Nice to see you! The Bruce Forsyth Story)

I Start Counting (1969) 105 mins

'You are a funny little biscuit.'

After viewing virtually every piece of film and television work that Jenny has acted in, I would not hesitate to say that I Start Counting is her best work thus far.

With a screenplay by telly writer Richard Harris (no, not that one) being an adaptation of the 1960s novel by Audrey Erskine Lindop, the film is a stupendous piece of work and a tour-de-force for the actress. Part blossoming of a young woman's sexuality, part psychological thriller, I Start Counting journeys through a terrific voyage of discovery by an exceedingly fresh-faced Jenny as Wynne, a 15-year-old. In actuality, she was 17 but director David Greene ably presents a believable world inhabited by such a young person wherein you are not yet an adult but no longer a child. Greene frames the scenes very adeptly and it is a good-looking feature.

Set in Bracknell, a designated 'new town' some 30 miles from London, I Start Counting has some similarities with another British film offering familial rites of passage: Gregory's Girl (1981). Both films show the daily life of a youngster growing up in a modern, faceless town burgeoning with development. And similar in many ways to the latter, I Start Counting opens with the camera P.O.V panning around the bedroom of a young girl (Jenny) in an establishing shot filled with the usual teen-aged accoutrements: school uniform, cuddly toy, hairbrush and so forth all visible. And just like gangling Gregory, we see Wynne (Jenny) getting ready for school clad in her uniform of white knee-length socks, grey jumper and tie and the mandatory short skirt ala Walkabout. It transpires that she has been adopted and lives with her step family in a new home distance away from the cosy cottage of their recent past. We have mum (Madge Ryan), gramps (Billy Russell) younger brother (Michael Feast, who acted with Jenny years later in an episode of Boon) and older brother George (Bryan Marshall) As the serene tones of the Lindsay Moore theme song cascades it is clear that the girl has a crush on her 32-year-old step brother (a rugged yet still tender turn by the RADA-trained Marshall) and cannot see anything bad in him at all. Even when it looks like he could be responsible for doing something very bad indeed her motivation is to try and help cover things up rather than believe the worst about him. In a touching, heart felt scene mid-way through the film, Jenny's character becomes intoxicated after drinking a bottle of beer and declares her previously unspoken desires to the much older sibling. The tension between them throughout is all handled very believably and it is clear that this affectation is all in her head but boy does she become infatuated.

Life for the pretty, shoulder-haired Wynne revolves around her school pal Corrine (a fizzing Clare Sutcliffe in a role with lots of false bravado and similar to Cassie Stuart in Secret Places) and lots of exaggerated conversations about boys. Even though both girls are physically mature, the pair are full of beans, both developing and pretty but frequently acting child-like as they tease and play off each other until ultimately being changed by the events that unfold.

Taking the local bus to and from school, the girls are often greeted by a cheeky un-named conductor portrayed by Simon Ward (looking very young indeed and from who more sinister thoughts will spring). Jenny would later appear with the appealing Mr.Ward in the 1970s spooky tale Dominique is Dead (1978). A series of sex murders of young woman still fails to deter the friends from the common (the scene of the crimes) or returning repeatedly to the condemned cottage where Wynn was once so content. It is whilst at the deserted house that her imagination flows freely and we literally see scenes played out from her mind: and not all pleasing.

The killings continue amidst local press headlines screaming 'Town of Fear' and 'Dalstead Common Murder' as the plot literally thickens and we wonder just who could be responsible: is it George or his younger brother or could it be the creepy ticket man? Lots of red herrings are planted as the drama hastens and rather than spoil its pulsating climax, I Start Counting concludes in a chase sequence with a sprinting Jenny being pursued by the killer, 'Oh! you shouldn't have come looking for her.' Quips the dastardly perpetrator. Directed by Manchester-born David Greene whose most fondly remembered work was the award-winning series Roots, I Start Counting was presented in cinemas by United Artists. Accommodating location shooting, the film makers also used Bray studios, home of the Hammer horror films of the 1950s-1960s. Ridiculously enough, this early Jenny feature was paired with war film Mosquito Squadron for its later cinema release back in the days when double-bills prevailed. Subsequently shown on television c.1980, I Start Counting has never been presented on DVD (or VHS, I believe) and is as allusive to get a hold of as the original Erskine-Lindop novel, which was one in a trio of her books to be turned into films.

The Railway Children (1970) 108 mins
'Keep off the tracks, Bobbie!'
From the opening scene in which Bobbie (Jenny) resplendent in a scarlet dress looks around the family living room accompanied by the first bar of the lovely music composed by Johnny Douglas, Lionel Jeffries immediately draws you into the world of the story about to be told: and we enter this willingly.
Jenny narrates as well and the big-screen adaptation is fittingly more lavish than the former BBC telly versions before it. As a popular comedy actor and burgeoning adapted-screenplay writer,

Jeffries has left behind him a wonderful piece with many similarities to another of his films, The Amazing Mr Blunden (1972). The Railway Children features many of the same supporting cast members and its story has parallels to the later film which also details the life of a struggling family without a father present. It is well-documented that Mr Jeffries did not set out to make a children's film, *per se*, and he spent 4 months adapting the E.Nesbitt book into a script. With a 300k budget, he binned the proposal of turning the story into a musical, muted by an American studio and by the time of making The Railway Children, he had acted in 100+ films. The idyllic family life of the Waterbury family is initially outlined before a 'dreadful change' occurs that realigns the lives of mother (Dinah Sheridan), father (Iain Cuthbertson, hamming it up madly), eldest daughter Roberta (Jenny), Phyllis (Sally Thomsett, who has quite a likeness to Clare Sutcliffe from I Start Counting) and Peter (Garry F.Warren). It is a film that you think you know but so much more is revealed after returning to it after a number of years away or a second viewing. As you might well know, father is mysteriously taken away and the family is uprooted from their comfortable dwelling at 'Edgecombe Villas' to a life in the country that initially proves quite a culture shock. Jeffries moves them to Yorkshire where the children immediately run of into the nearby fields (Jenny jumps over the camera positioned on the ground at one point in a lovely, dreamy sequence) and explore their new environment. With birds a-tweeting, just as in Blunden, the harshness towards children is briefly hinted at but their mother always shelters them and allows them to express themselves freely (to the chagrin of related-adults upon occasion).

'Three chimneys' becomes their new home and today the property is privately-owned but a public footpath runs past it if you fancy taking a look. Outside, that iconic fence upon which the trio perch upon to wave down at passing trains now only partly remains. As with the BBC series that Jenny was also involved in, the wooden fence is a place they often return to. The screenplay obviously does differ in some ways between the film and the original book and examples of this will be commented upon shortly.

Oakworth is the local train station where the youngsters first meet 'dear Mr Perks', the station porter. In the telly adaptation the station master features but in the film 'his nibbs' is only referenced in passing by the Vaudevillian turn so perfectly made manifest by Bernard Cribbins. Jeffries incorporates a familiar trick of playing the same bit of music each time the former appears; all frantic and fast! Born in 1928, Cribbins was the narrator of the 'Tufty' British Public Information Films of the 1970s and The Wombles telly series. Still acting nowadays, with a recent project being Doctor Who, he has been performing since the age of 14. Hugely popular on telly and film across many, many years he worked with Sid James, Peter Sellers and Jeffries on a number of British films. (As for Mr.Jeffries, he does not seem to have appeared in anything since 2001).

Perks is an earnest and proud working man married with lots of children and a wife portrayed by Blunden actress Deddie Davies. He and his brood strike a mutually-warm relationship. Young master Peter (Warren) eyes up the coal stored at the station and re-assigns it to his mother's fire but his subsequent 'capture' by Perks is not seen.

Jenny was eighteen when the Railway Children was released and Sally Thomsett, as younger sister 'Phyl' was actually a couple of years older than her screen sibling! As 'Lanky', Jenny and her sister are again all smocks and hats-at-the-back-of-the-head wearers whilst their brother shares similar characteristics to the young lad James from The Amazing Mr Blunden. I think the same could be said for Jenny as with the Lynne Frederick young lady in the latter film: all earnest sincerity and having to take on maternal/ adult responsibilities.

Returning to the story, all three children talk about the whereabouts of their absent father and agree to send their love via the passing London-bound train each day (thinking that he might be in the city somewhere). That's where the waving comes into play and at first only one person seems to respond; an older gentleman. Portrayed in the film by William Mervyn and in the 2000 telly version by

Sir Richard Attenborough, he returns their greetings and becomes an intricate part of their lives as the story develops. When mother becomes ill, the children ask their 'old gentleman' if he could obtain the exotic, vitamin-enriched items that Dr. Forrest (portrayed by Peter Bromilow but oddly said to have had his voice dubbed) recommends to aid her recovery. They have no money but pass a note to the gent and are delighted to receive a hamper full of goods for their ailing parent. A proud woman (we never get to know what her actual name is) she berets the children for allowing others to know their private family business before stating that she will personally thank him for his kindness.) Mervyn, by then a vastly experienced television actor and used to waiting about on sets, had quite an effect upon the locals used as extras during the production; even inviting them all for a drink at a nearby pub on one occasion. He died in 1976.

In a lovely, dream-like scene Bobbie's birthday is acknowledged by her family and close adult friends (not once do the children interact with local youngsters) in a deliciously surreal sequence. As she tearfully greets and thanks each person, Jenny literally glides amongst them and let's allow Lionel Jeffries to explain just how he achieved a very peculiar effect. 'She sat on the camera stool and I was underneath. He remembered in the BBC documentary I Love a 1970s Christmas. 'With the music we moved with it and the tears that were pouring down the crew's eyes when we cut it...!' Both Bernard Cribbins and Sally Thomsett contributed to that show but not Jenny. It is quite moving but also quite a trippy, on-screen moment. As with the book and previous small-screen adaptations of it, the story moves on to the seemingly unwelcomed arrival of a Russian dissident that somehow finds himself at Oakworth station. The children again call on the guidance of the old gentleman who manages to re-unite the man, whom it is revealed is a famous writer, with his family. Immediately after, the exciting landslide scene appears on screen and it is done with much aplomb. 'They won't see us. It's all no good!' exhales a worried Bobbie as the steam from an on-coming loco billows from around the corner before the massive engine roars towards where some trees have fallen onto the line. Here Nesbitt's red petticoats moment comes into play as Ms.Thomsett's Phyl (described fondly in the novel as a 'silly cuckoo' by her brother) has the smart idea to wave them as a warning sign of the impending danger. Atypically, the younger children squabble as to who is in charge whilst Roberta looks on as the train edges dangerously nearer. Thankfully the driver sees them and halts the loco literally in front of the brave Bobbie's nose! She faints as the danger peaks before her and our very own eyes. It's a great moment and was filmed just the once during a searing summer using a fibre-glass tree made by the props department at Elstree studios (it languished in the Oakworth yard for many years after the film was made). That scene is not historically correct in that petticoats were not worn in the period which the story is set so clearly; it being acknowledged by academics that Nesbit is using as a reference to the past.

The children's bravery is publically acknowledged by a 'thank you' ceremony and another Jeffries co-hort, David Lodge, features as a bemused bandleader constantly thwarted by musicians that cannot play in time! When they do manage it, the crowd has moved on. The year of 1905 is acknowledged and the youngsters all look splendid in their best bonnets and suits. In the 1968 telly version, mother does not appear at the event but Jeffries chooses to include her in his cinematic version.

A beautiful shot of the 4 family members returning home in the early summer evening sunshine is one of many handsome moments provided by the cine-matographer/ director of photography Arthur Ibbetson.

Cribbins and his on-screen wife play well together in the film and Perks seems to be a role that every actor portraying him manages to bring much warmth too. A credit to the rich writing skills of Edith Nesbit here I feel.

Bobbie receives quite a shock upon discovering the truth about her missing father (he has been imprisoned as a spy) after their trusty porter offers the children some unwanted newspapers from the station waiting room. And again the paper chase scene is included with the tiny 'Phyl' cannily observing the burning affect that the young lad has had upon her older sister as he leaves with the old gentleman (it transpires that he is his nephew: some sharp plotting here by the author).

Once more Roberta takes on the burden of asking the gentleman for his measurable assistance relating to her father's political plight. And again he is able to make things change for the better. This man should have become the Prime Minister as he does so much good in this story.

Just when we think that perhaps the film is over, more than 90 minutes in, we see the three youngsters return to their fence and acknowledge their debt to the railway. They decide to wave to the next passing train and are amazed to see each and every passenger enthusiastically return their greetings including their old gentleman being in his usual seat back in the rear carriage.

Moments later, Bobbie and her siblings are in the midst of a home lesson with their mother when the elder child feels the need to be alone. Her understanding parent allows her to go off and so Bobbie decides to visit Perks at the station. The trainman is full of beans and seems to know something that she does not. Congratulating her on the 'news', a bemused Bobbie has no idea of what is about to happen to her. A train approaches with much dramatic steam (rather a lot but we can allow the director this) eventually clearing with a

figure remaining on the platform. The dawning realisation comes to her and that classic line of 'Daddy, my daddy!' is uttered as Jenny runs towards him and he lifts her off her feet. Effectively, the camera freeze frames and allows the intensity of the moment to pour out prior to them walking back to the family home. 'When you read the book it is so extraordinary. I think that Lionel Jeffries did capture it exceptionally well.' Recounted Jenny in a recent BBC television interview. From the bedroom window above, mother sees them approach before he motions into the house whilst Bobbie remains outside. The other children come into the scene and are informed by their sister that father has returned but that the parents must be allowed a private moment together. I, for one, always found her understanding of this to be rather irritating but such is her character's sensitivity. In the novel the author speaks directly to the reader and tells us about what is happening but she says that she will not follow the family indoors after father returns.

Just as in The Amazing Mr Blunden, for the closing credits, Jeffries lines up his main actors (in front of a train in this instance) as the camera approaches and the cast waves and smiles to us, the audience. It is a lovely touch and proves an endearing and fitting conclusion. A close-up sees a giggling Jenny revealing a small blackboard with 'The End' written over it and a smile breezes across the face whether you realise it not.

Shot on location in Yorkshire and utilising studio space at Elstree, Jenny remains complimentary about Jeffries and a wonderful film remains to be enjoyed by all ages.

After the picture was released Jenny did various theatre and film work before Logan's Run was to make her a star in America. As for he screen siblings, Warren went on to appear in the Catweazle series before subsequently leaving the acting profession in the late-1970s. He now works in the London clothing trade. Sally Thomsett was 20 when she portrayed Phyllis, a girl meant to be half that age in the film and her shining performance was recognised by her nomination for a prestigious Most Promising Newcomer film award. Diametrically opposed to her appearance in The Railway Children, she is also remembered for being dizzy blonde Jo in telly comedy Man About the House (1973-6).

Jenny's onscreen parents in the film, Iain Cuthbertson and Dinah Sheridan had both been in the business for some years when acting in The Railway Children. Cuthebertson, a giant Glasgow-born actor with a massively diverse career taking in hard man Charlie Endell in Budgie, forever battering a long-haired Adam Faith (later of Love Hurts fame in which Jenny would play a recurring character). As well as lots of children's telly roles as diverse as Super Gran to Dr Who. The beautiful Miss. Sheridan mainly worked on television after co-starring in classic British films such as Genevieve (1953) and with Nigel Havers in the insipid Don't Wait Up from 1983-90. Curiously, Dinah's first stage role was in a touring company production of Peter Pan. And of course, Jenny would herself feature in a version of the play many years later.

Locations used for the film include the following:

1. Oakworth Station - home to Mr Perks the porter and the scene of many adventures for Roberta, Phyllis and Peter. The booking hall was used in the film to take the distressed Russian into and the ladies waiting room was used as Perks' office. See the photo of Jenny on the contents page for a shot taken of her in a recent return visit to the station.
2. Dr Forrest's surgery/ home are easily recognisable as the famous Bronte Parsonage at the top of Haworth's Main Street.
3. Scenes showing Bobbie sitting on a bridge near a river were filmed at Wycoller, near Colne.
4. The cutting where the children wave to the train is located on the Haworth side of Mytholmes tunnel. If you look up the bank just before the tunnel, you can still see part of the original fence where they sat and waved at passing trains.
5. The landslide sequence was filmed on the left bank in the cutting below the Oakworth side of Mytholmes tunnel.
6. The section of line between Mytholmes tunnel and Oakworth station (known as Mytholmes Curve) was where the two girls waved their red flannel petticoats to stop the train running into the unseen landslide.
7. Mytholmes tunnel between Haworth and Oakworth was used for the paper chase scenes. This is where Tom injured his leg and was rescued

by the three 'Railway children'.

8. The fields of long grass which they are seen running through to wave to the trains are located on the hillside just above Oxenhope station. This location was used in conjunction with the one near Mytholmes Tunnel (see previous) where the wooden fence is positioned.

9. Mr Perks cottage stands next to the level crossing at Oakworth station. The building was extended several years ago - the white part is the original building - but is still recognisable as the family home of the friendly porter.

10. A family picnic by the river - this idyllic scene is thought to have been filmed in the fields at Mytholmes, near Bridgehouse Beck.

11. Bent's Farm just above Oxenhope station featured as 'Three Chimneys'. This is now a private house but a public footpath runs up the hillside close by. The fields below the house were used in several scenes.

Trains play a major part in The Railway Children and the release of the film benefited the Keighley & Worth Valley Railway (known as the K&WVR) tremendously, immediately increasing the number of visitors to the area seen in the film from 60k to 150k. In autumn 1969, future director Lionel Jeffries and his production staff examined the line to see if it would be suitable for location filming. They would need to utilise a station, a number of trains, a long tunnel and more all within a certain area and the K&WVR fitted the bill to a tee.

(Their line at the time was the only one in the country that could easily accommodate such needs.) Members from the line were delighted upon managing to persuade the film makers to retain the Oakworth station name for inclusion in their story thus allowing the piece to boost visitors to the area: it worked, as the above figures ably demonstrate.

As for the handsome trains seen in the film, 'The Green Dragon' (as Phyllis describes it) is still in use on the line today following a major refurbishment. The sumptuous wooden carriage used by the 'old gentleman' is still in operation and occasionally seen on the line nowadays. The train that featured in the pivotal return of the Waterbury's father at the end of the film is still around but now in use in Leeds.

For publicity purposes, and incorporated into the end of the film where the cast waves at the camera, was the steam locomotive called 'Lord Mayor'. (A still of it with the cast appeared on the front cover of the Puffin novel tie-in, see picture elsewhere). In 2005 the National Railway Museum in York marked the centenary of the book with a special 'Railway Children' exhibition. In mid-2009 a live theatrical performance of the story returned to the museum wherein the audience sat in carriage-type seats to watch the performance. Filming for the big screen version of The Railway Children commenced in April 1969 and ran for some 39 location days and a further 15 in the studios at Elstree. It was reported that the finished project premiered in London in December 1970 and that it was awarded a Royal premiere at which the audience stood and applauded! The American film poster summed its appeal up concisely commending it as being a film for 'adults to take their children, too!' Jenny's film also played at the Keighley Ritz cinema shortly after and continues to bring visitors to the area to re-visit the locations so beautifully captured in the film.

A beguiling Jenny was interviewed briefly by the Yorkshire TV show 'Calendar News' and features a costumed Jenny talking about the production.
'There are lots of adventures that happen to them.' Remarked the demure Ms.Agutter whilst on location for the film.

Nearly 40 years since the film was released Jenny is still associated with the work and has returned to Oakworth a number of times in support of the Cystic Fibrosis Trust and the K&WVR line itself. She also contributed a foreword to The Illustrated Railway Children [published by Kettering/ Silver link in 2005] and always has to talk about it when promoting current or recent acting projects. It is also known that she has long since been developing a biography film about Edith Nesbit. A commemorative plaque was placed at the station in 1996 to celebrate the centenary of British cinema and the film association with the place itself. In 2000, the Derbyshire village of New Mills contested the inspiration for Nesbitt's work stating that they possessed all the necessary elements utilised for the story and claiming that the author had been known to visit the area prior to writing The Railway Children.

Critical comments:
'There are few films that provoke reviewers into using the word "perfect," but this film deserves the term. It's hard to imagine how Nesbit's beautiful children's story could have been told with any greater sensitivity for all of its potential.'
(Ref: metalluk / Epinions.com)
'Much of the film's success depends on the trio of children. Eldest is played with grave confidence by snub-nosed Jenny Agutter.'
(Ref: Variety Movie guide, 1999)

Walkabout (1971) 95 mins

'Strangers in a strange land…a primitive world where nature and civilization collide.' The 1998 Video/ DVD release copyline.
'The Aborigine and the girl 30,000 years apart…together.' Text from the original film poster featuring a shot of a nude Jenny swimming in a scene from the movie.

Helmed by first-time director Nic Roeg, then a cinematographer who combines both duties on the film, Walkabout was shot entirely on location in Australia. With an adapted screenplay by Edward Bond of the original novel by James Vance Marshall, Walkabout was a film that I viewed again recently after seeing it as a youngster some years after its original release. It was with some trepidation that I re-watched the opening explanation that a 'Walkabout' is a rites of passage tradition for every native Australian i.e. sixteen-year-old Aborigine males. They are cast off to fend for themselves in the harsh, beautiful outback where only the strongest or the most industrious will survive.

Not that this was the cause of my consternation, it was the number of naturalistic scenes intercut within the narrative that I for one found disturbing. And watching the film again, the moments which feature the killing of animas and survival struggles, retain their horrid affect upon the viewer. Now I understand the film makers reasoning behind the inclusion of such brutal imagery but it still disturbs.

However, the memory of a very beautiful Jenny within Walkabout has made the film intrinsically linked to her screen persona with fans and public alike. She is top-billed as the 'white girl' next to her little screen brother, the excellent Lucien John (aka Nic Roeg's son) and the 'black boy' as portrayed by David Gumpilil.

Within the first ten minutes, Roeg perfectly places the contrast of Sydney city life (all cars, concrete, bricks and mortar) with the soon-to-be explored desert of the outback. It is clear that the teenaged Jenny and her 4 or 5 year-old brother are from a moneyed background: both being uniformed in public school attire of blazers and hats.

Our first impression of Jenny, playing a fourteen-year-old, is certainly influenced by the thigh-length skirt that she wears although it was the end of the 1960s and into the next decade such attire would remain on the short side (see I Start Counting, also). Still, the story is definitely marking out a distinction that this is a blossoming young lady (which it continues to do so oftenly and throughout). An unnerving moment sees the father (an excellent John Meillon) take the 2 youngsters out of town and into the arid edge of the outback where a transparent undercurrent lingers with all eyes on her svelte body. Little is said between the man and young woman even when Jenny's character sets up a picnic outside the VW Beetle car that has just brought them there. Interestingly, the boy terms him as their father but she never does. A truly disturbing scene then takes place whereby he begins to shoot at them before turning the gun on himself after setting fire to the vehicle. It's a shocking moment as although he is seen focusing upon some paperwork the viewer could never guess at what is to come. It shakes everything up and proves the catalyst for the siblings to make their own odyssey.

The 'outback,' undefeated by development, immediately fills the screen with an infusion of brown, orange and greens via some evocative photography. Walkabout was the final film project within which Roeg would perform the latter solely and he is quoted as saying that he could not imagine relying upon others for this attribute. The images are complimented by the sumptuous John Barry soundtrack, with the environment soon swallowing the youngsters up into its vastness. Miss Agutter, of whom it has been well-documented, has a great fondness for Australia, features in another role involving a younger sibling. The Railway Children immediately springs to mind, with the BBC serial that she first appeared in back in 1968 and of course, the 1970 feature film classic.

Brother and sister begin to wilt in the intense sun on their second day outside and at half-hour into the film, the Aborigine boy first shows himself. It is upon his introduction that Jenny's young lady produces that wretched dictum of 'We're British!' to the non-English foreigner and you do squirm at this moment. As portrayed by Gumpilil, this future award-winning Aborigine actor continues to act and most recently starred in the Nicole Kidman epic, Australia (2008). Jenny would return 'down under' to attend his subsequent This is your Life style show many years later. As for Lucien, the young boy, he really puts in an endearing performance and now works as a producer with Walkabout his only acting experience regrettably. Some crude sexual imagery pervades as the white brother and sister accompany the young native. And just under an hour of screen time, the infamous nude swimming scene occurs and it really is framed delightfully right: coming across

as quite natural. The director shot the sequence with a tele-photo lens from some distance away and reassured Jenny that it would work out fine. Therefore, the audience does not feel as if it is peeping at her. Although the moment is graphically juxtaposed by the hideous slaughter of a kangaroo which is awful to see. This is just one of a number of gruesome deaths on screen which however indigineous to the location, does affect the viewer. The journey being almost over, the young boy tells his sister of the discovery of a nearby road after they have travelled long and hard. It is here that is the location for the end for one of the group. Their voyage literally almost over, or beginning if you see it that way, a return to city dwelling provokes a flashback for Jenny. This comes in the form of an extended return to the water scene of earlier only with all 3 youngsters laughing and enjoying themselves in their natural state. The symbolism of their school hats and blazers contrast well with the feral nature of the Australian outback and the closing imagery succinctly defines the passing of their own rites of passage. Exceptional fare but with some distressing real-life brutality.

Since appearing in the film both Jenny and Lucien Roeg featured in the Channel 4 documentary '50 films to see before you die (2006).' A restored version of Walkabout was said to have been released in the late-1990s with the added sequence following the brief encounter between the Aborigine boy and a nubile young woman, whom

by James Vance Marshall

he ignores before moving on with the others. Apparently featuring an extra scene where the woman is in bed alone whilst her partner teaches painting to Aborigine children. This side of the scene is not present in non-American film prints. A 2008 screening on Channel 5 in Britain presented a much-maligned edit with some nudity and animal slaughter/ suicide imagery removed, it caused much consternation with puzzled viewers unaware that it was said to be the cinematic version released in cinemas back in the 1970s. Critical comments:

'…a superb work of storytelling and effortlessly fascinating…'
(Ref: film critic Roger Ebert)
'Absorbing at face value, disturbing underneath. It isn't perfect, but when it works, it's brilliant, and a definite recommendation for viewers looking for something a little more challenging than your typical adventure film.
(Ref: Vince Leo)
'One of the most original, visually stunning, and provocative films of the 1970s…timeless in its beauty and unique approach to a classic coming-of-age story…arguably Roeg's finest achievement.'
(Ref: www.toptenreviews.com)
'…a director's and photographer's experimental success.'
(Ref: film critic Leslie Halliwell)
'An extraordinary film.' Jenny Agutter
left: the 1973 Penguin/ Peacock tie-in paperback.

The Snow Goose (1971) 60 mins

'A friend to all things wild and the wild things repaid him with their friendship.'

Possibly by the time that you are reading this the remake of this original made-for-TV film may well have been released. The best-selling novella written by a former American sports writer, Paul Gallico, struck a chord with a war-torn culture and sold more than a half million copies within weeks of being published in 1941. His simple tale of the touching relationship between an isolated man, played by Richard Harris and a young girl played by Jenny, in the desolate marshlands of the Essex coast was shown on television in December 1971. It took 6 weeks to film and saw Harris return to a small-screen role after many years away.

Gallico lived in Britain for a time and the casting of Harris as the weathered Phillip and Jenny as Frith (Fritha) proves wholly endearing. The film, highly sort after by its many admirers today (I don't think that it has ever been commercially released) was directed by Patrick Garland with a script being an adaptation of his own work by the author. The finished piece won many awards: Gallico for his screen adaptation, an American Emmy for Jenny, and indeed for its lovely cinematography and its editing.

Harris was nominated for a Golden Globe for his initially irritating, whispering interpretation amongst a trio of other nominations for the film itself (and Garland for his direction). The Snow

opposite: the 1978 Penguin book tie-in novel of The Snow Goose.

THE SNOW GOOSE

Paul Gallico's moving classic of Dunkirk.
Also containing
THE SMALL MIRACLE

Goose is clearly a work of some stature and is much-loved by its fans and readers of the novel. Resembling the UK equivalent of Grizzly Addams, that original hell raiser, Richard Harris, saw his lengthy career incorporate Camelot (1967) and King George II in Jenny's King of the Wind (1990). He is very good here but does have a tendency to whisper his dialogue. Gallico's description of his screen character is quite sharp: a hunch back with one hand missing and an 'ugly man' not liked by the local villagers (yet he bares them no malice).

In the book, Jenny's Frith is stated to be 'no more than twelve' when the story begins and it covers a number of years through to the mass Dunkirk evacuations of 1940. That historical event, when the British government requested that all merchant/ private boats and crafts help in the enormously hasty evacuation of stranded British troops on that bloody beach, plays a fateful part in the story.

An artist and nature-lover, *par excellence*, Phillip (Harris) first meets Frith when a lost Canadian snow goose is injured by the buckshot of a reckless hunter. The two work together in the rehabilitation of the beautiful bird at the defunct lighthouse at which he has made his home (The film makers constructed the building on location in Frinton, on the east coast of England).

In the novel, Frith brings the bird to the desolate light house but in the film they meet out on the marshes immediately after the bird is hit. There are a number of small changes from page to screen and I would recommend reading the book first. Jenny may well be portraying a 'little girl' but she was actually 18 at the time of filming. So clearly, she does look somewhat older than the young girl being portrayed but this has been a regular occurrence for Jenny and many others so let's not be overly-critical. When we first see her on screen, Jenny wears a peak cap and has her hair in braids. In the book, the period of time covered is made much clearer as we trace their relationship via the migratory habits of the wild fowl that travel across the Essex marshlands. In the film I found the time scale less well-defined and the undercurrent of tension between the two characters is less pronounced. If you read the novel after seeing the film, you may well be shocked to understand the unspoken love experienced by these two disparate people.

A simple example is demonstrated in the film when Jenny dashes off after Phillip looks at her in that specific way.

Their association is ruled by the annual migration patterns of the birds and there are big gaps in-between times when they do not see each other. This is when Phillip works on a stunning painting of an incandescent young Frith holding their beloved snow goose whence they first met. Time passes and Jenny's innocent young scamp blossoms into a young woman and in Gallico's novel, their unspoken feelings seem in no way inappropriate but the film does not have such transparency. The fowl becomes tame and after flying away one season returns later much to the delight of both, 'It's a miracle Frith, a miracle,' exhorts an excited Phillip.

Harris rightly enjoyed a career that spanned a number of decades and what comes across in The Snow Goose is the connection that these two people make through their love of nature and the simple fact that they are both alone. Other differences between the book and film include the localized dialect spoken by Frith but in the latter, Jenny has only an indication of an accent.

As mentioned earlier, the war quite literally invades the isolated marshes when a German plane is seen flying nearby as Phillip and Frith are enjoying some time together. This develops as he joins the throng of more than 800 sailing boats in the evacuation of Dunkirk and the book differs in its description of these events by using other characters to re-tell these moments. Frith begs him not to go and pleads that she accompany him but his boat is so small that he cannot spare the space. You almost feel that he is not going to return and Jenny shows this too. I will not give away the ending other than to say that the final scene sees Jenny's Frith return to the lighthouse and see the snow goose fly by as she takes the portrait and leaves. After passing away in 1976, the rights to this film seem to have passed on to the estate of Paul Gallico and are co-owned by Hallmark Hall of Fame. This American company co-produced the film with the BBC and confusion abounds as to why this wonderful work has not received an official DVD release. The Estate says that they have no objections to its release and it is for Hallmark to do what they wish with it. Other sources say the opposite. Who knows the actual truth but it seems a great shame that an author who resisted numerous attempts to turn his novella into a film until agreeing to this production, should now see it unavailable.

Critical comments:

'An extraordinary movie…Richard Harris and Jenny Agutter were perfect in their respective parts. The setting, the music, the actors, the writing, all superb.'
(REF: marianna1776/ nytimes.com)

A War of Children (1972) 73 mins

'People over here seem to think if you wear a uniform you are some kind of enemy, or murderer: or both.' Harry Andrews in the film.

Set amidst the 'troubles' of Belfast in 1972 (although Dublin was used to double for the city) this made-for-TV feature won an American Emmy award for Best Outstanding Single Programme and was also nominated for a Golden Globe (both 1973). Its American director George Schaeffer also received an Emmy nomination for this engaging story written by James Costigan, himself a triple Emmy winner and established TV and occasional film screenplay author.

Vivian Merchant and John Ronane play the Catholic parents of Maureen and Donal (Jenny and the delightful Danny Figgis) whose friendship with a Protestant family is tested to the brink amidst the fear and prejudice of life in the ugly sectarian Ireland of the period.

Jenny appears on screen immediately and looks radiant as a young woman who becomes involved with a British soldier (played by a debutant Harry Andrews with an exaggerated 'London' accent). Harry worked with Jenny associates John Gielgud and Michael York and is best-remembered for his roles in the Brideshead Revisted and Danger UXB telly serials. However, this is where the problem lays with A War of Children, in the differing Irish (or 'Oirrish') accents adopted by the actors. None of them sound as if they are actually from Northern Ireland and although the youngster playing Robbie, the son in the Protestant family (David G.Meredith) is endearing, he sounds English most of the time. It makes one think of those middle class actors that played working class characters in any number of British-made features from the 1930s onwards. It does detract from the authenticity of the piece which blends in reportage footage of actual bombings and its after-effects with the fictional story presented on screen. The 2nd unit toured about Dublin backstreets for stock film footage and even took a hidden camera into Belfast during its 4 week location filming.

Jenny received an exclusive 'Special guest appearance' credit for her sensitive role as Maureen Tomulty and she looks very pretty. A particularly affecting moment sees her and Reg (Andrews) discovered after sleeping together for the first time, by a braying mob of women, one of whom is her own mother (Merchant). Maureen has her long hair brutally hacked at by her parent prior to enduring the indignity of being ceremoniously 'tarred and feathered' by the gang. Peculiarly enough, seeing Jenny immediately after this scene prompts the viewer to think of her character from East of Sudan.

Somewhat clumsily acted at times, and with glaring plot contrivances, A War of Children is still worth a look for Jenny fans and I especially liked master Figgis as her younger brother. Regrettably, he only acted in one other project and coinciden-tally it had John Gielgud in its cast (see The Tempest, in the theatre section). This film was held as a second, supporting feature release by British Lion Films after being entered as the Irish entry in the Cork Film festival. It was originally to be a television presentation but was awarded the chance of a cinema release as an 'A' certificate.

Critical comments:

'If the film itself is offensively simple the appeal to the emotions through the contrivance of its plot is blatant enough to hold the attention. Jenny Agutter…enters into the star crossed spirit of the occasion with every sign of sincerity.'

(Ref: Eric Shorter, Daily Telegraph, 15 April 1973)

Logan's Run (1976) 118 mins

'Welcome to the 23rd century. The perfect world of total pleasure…there's just one catch…'

Film tagline

The opening shot in the film begins with a very poor looking plastic exterior representation of a city inhabited by Jenny and others. By today's CGI-infused standard it looks feeble: all the exteriors being seen as exactly what they are - models! Writing in his autobiography, even lead actor Michael York acknowledged the fact that the SFX are pretty dire. But for the time, Logan's Run utilised the best of what was available and its technical endeavours were oddly rewarded via an Academy Award for Special Effects. Logan was also nominated for the Golden Prize in the 1980 Moscow Film Festival and was once screened to an audience at an athletics stadium there.

A rightly bland York stars as Logan 5, a 'sand man,' one of the elite policemen-type enforcers within the sanitised city whose job is to terminate those that run once their life clock, secreted in the palm of their left hand, begins flashing. He and co-hort Richard Jordan are good at their job and seem to enjoy the chase: strange because the city is said to be focussed upon pleasure up until the inhabitants reach 30 years of age. Then things turn sour: an event called 'Carousel' beckons and most of the people who go there are killed/ terminated. Carousel is where those selected are basically zapped to death whilst an enraptured audience enjoys the show! Director Michael Anderson, later to direct Jenny in Dominique is Dead (1978) said that the Coliseum in Rome was his inspiration for these scenes. Anderson enjoyed his daily involvement on set and was excited at the possibilities presented as to what the production was attempting to achieve. Innumerable technical experts were involved in constructing the 21st century world and all its wonders.

At 15 minutes in: Jenny is literally beamed in by Michael York who selects her for sexual gratification after she makes herself available. He doesn't get what he wants as she is troubled by more serious issues. Jenny looks very appealing in a light green, bra-less outfit that is little more than a piece of lightly placed material ! The two become interested in each other and the nasal-sounding York seeks her insider knowledge when he is forced to become a 'Runner' by the faceless authorities, losing 4 years of his lifespan as a consequence (as you have to be 30). Logan speaks with her as part of his secret mission to find 'Sanctuary' a mythical place where those that fight against Carousel seek by hiding within the contours of the city and its hazardous, off-limit zones.

27 minutes in: Jenny reappears and takes Logan into the 'cathedral' zone, a so-called 'reservation for violent delinquents'; a lawless area not controlled by the powers-that-be. The late Farah Fawcett featured in a pre-Charlie's Angels role here, employed at a department where city inhabitants visit for rejuvenating plastic surgery. Logan is almost killed as both Farah and the surgeon (played by the son of the director) fear his motivation. 'Sandmen never run!' offers a doubter.

One hour in: sees Michael and Jenny having to run together after she discovers his plans to find Sanctuary (she doesn't yet realize that he is under-cover). The excellent Richard Jordan (Francis) now turns from friend to hunter as he seeks to terminate them both. Francis struggles to accept his friend's justifications throughout the story and even when he is killed, his dying moments still do not betray his indoctrinated state of there being no life outside of the domed city. A scene thereabouts sees the two 'runners' almost drown in a torrent of water which the actors agreed to appear in, despite the obvious dangers (stunt performers were used for the distanced shots).

Continuing on and following lots of running and swimming, the duo arrive at a frozen land outside of their known environment. Resplendent with frozen penguin and walrus sculptures or at least that is what we think they are, they meet a ridiculous silver robot called 'Box'. Looking as realistic as a 1970s Dr Who cyborg, 'Box' tries to kill the two of them after it is revealed that this is actually his job description! That and the collection of frozen people all stored in a row as a terrified York and Jenny gradually realise the true nature of the place. They are not about to be freeze-dried and destroy the cyborg and all around them as the bemused Francis follows on behind. 'Box' was voiced and played by Roscoe Lee Browne, a Vincent Price sound-a-like and turns quite sinister after initially welcoming the couple. An establishing scene involving them posing for him was cut from the final film.

Nearly 70 minutes into the story: Logan and Jessica (Jenny) are amazed at being outside of their protected home and experience the wonder of seeing the sun for the first time although they do not know what it is. Bruised and battered they march on still seeking to find sanctuary whilst their love for each other is reciprocated. Jenny and Michael do a spot of skinny dipping ala Walkabout prior to walking towards a deserted, overgrown city: Washington D.C. There they discover the Lincoln memorial and are puzzled by the weathered features of the former president. Both Michael and Jenny's characters are intriguing when they are confronted by sights that they have no experience of, as is the appealing Jordan as a fellow Sandman.

This is further developed when they meet an old man portrayed by a cheeky Peter Ustinov. It seems that he is the only survivor of a nuclear holocaust and both youngsters are puzzled by his explanation of his parents' involvement in his life. Michael York puts in a suitably plain performance but holds his deceit well from Jenny. He still does not disclose his real reasons for instigating his journey but things turn nasty with the re-emergence of Francis and a heavily-choreographed fight between the former friends. Just before, Logan decrees that Sanctuary does not exist to a furious Jessica (Jenny) who wants to keep on going forward. All such matters are suspended as the fight concludes with the death of Francis. I think that many of us find his character's journey of equal interest to that of the York / Agutter axis. Acting roles for Jordan came the way of the personable American actor from the 1960s after which point he would gain valuable experience as a theatre performer/writer and producer. He died in 1993.

Returning to the story, Ustinov provides some almost misplaced humour in his scenes, indulging in much improvisation with the agreement of Anderson, after the two had previously worked together on another film. Sounding like and having the mannerisms of the Cowardly lion from the Wizard of Oz, Ustinov's involvement proves significant for the oncoming climax of the story.

Interestingly, James Cagney was approached to play the part but turned it down as he had retired (but he was in fact later to return to film). Mr Ustinov died in 2004 when Jenny was quoted by the BBC, remembering him as an 'extraordinarily wonderful person to work with.'

Logan wants to return to the city to tell all those within it that people do live to an old age and that they should believe it as he speaks the truth. But you know that this will prove all too much for the drone-like inhabitants who have known nothing else other than the artifice of the city.

They do decide to return but leave the elderly gent (Ustinov) outside as they have to complete an arduous swim to get back in to the city confines. Throughout her career Jenny has had to be competent in a number of areas from riding a horse and trap, swimming and lots of physical stuff too. So finally, as some of the city dwellers head towards another wretched Carousel, Logan screams at them to acknowledge that life does continue after 30 and all they have to do is come and see the old man for proof. Logan and Jenny are recaptured but a final interrogation by the body-less voice of authority proves cataclysmic as his incalculable answers about his external discoveries cause the system to overload. Chaos ensues as the city literally and metaphorically collapses all around whilst the people flee outside for the first time and discover the truth upon seeing the seasoned Ustinov.

Logan's Run is a great adventure with the viewer

wishing the presented film to be more than the sum of its parts. Perhaps the re-imagining of the original novel with the advent in CGI et al will make the vision of the novel more malleable? Quoted on his website (see references) co-author William H.Nolan commented in 2001, 'M.G.M's Logan's Run is not Nolan/ Johnson's Logan's Run. Perhaps from Warner Bros. Who knows? Only time, and the new movie will give us the answers.' Jenny received third-billing in the film for which its original screenplay was written by the Nolan/ Johnson team back in the mid-1960s before being optioned by M.G.M in 1966 (in a shortened version). By this time the Kansas-born Nolan was a full-time writer and Johnson would enjoy a very eclectic career taking in television, novels and even acting. Now in his 80s, the latter continues to be creative whilst Nolan has more than 75 books on his CV (including 2 sequels to Logan's Run: Logan's World & Logan's Search: all 3 being available as part of a collected trilogy).

Ms.Agutter has termed the film as an adventure story wherein in 'the society is geared towards pleasure. So that everybody is happy and content.' That is of course, only a surface summation for beneath the laid back life in the domed city there is a far from savoury undercurrent. Her co-star, Michael York, also a trained actor with the National Theatre as would Jenny, defined Logan's Run as 'a fantastic journey through a world beyond imagination.' Michael has enjoyed a steady working career since the early-1960s and reveals in his autobiography that he did not want to even read the script initially. He was persuaded to do so and chose to make a break from the usual stuffed-shirt roles that he was cast for.

Logan's Run commenced filming in June 1975 and Jenny was involved from the first day. A scheduled shooting period of 2.5 months would incorporate 3 weeks in Dallas where the film makers utilised the still-new facilities of a giant shopping mall. The city seen in the film is actually the inner mall and its 1.8m sq feet floor space is used well. The nearby Fort Worth was home for the scenes where Jenny and Michael are seen immediately outside of the sanitised city (they have to dive into the water to enter/ exit).

The film of Logan's Run, much like Star Wars a couple of years later, produced many commercial spin-offs including jigsaws, lunchboxes, coffee mugs, tie-in novel as well as a six issue run of a comic produced by Marvel in May '77 with illustrated versions of Jenny and Michael on its cover. A year after its release a television show aired but with no involvement from Jenny. But to return to the root of the project: i.e. the Nolan and George Clayton Johnson novel continues to be in print more than 30 years since the film. Some 17 publishers and even an e-book has been produced in what Michael York was right about back in the 1970s in stating that the whole thing had become a cult. Jenny has featured on the cover art of the following film tie-ins:

1. Bantam (1976) - the official novel to accompany the release of the movie, pictured opp.

2. A Victor Gollancz hardback was published in 1976 with the added strap line of 'Now a spectacular MGM film' on its cover.

3. Corgi Books produced the British paperback to accompany the film upon its theatrical release.

4. A Spanish paperback printed in 1985 had a photographic cover of a wet-clothed Jenny & Michael from the film.

5. A 1977 Japanese hardback cover, beautifully designed, used stills from the film with Jenny & Michael holding hands with the city behind them.

Critical comments:

'…still a classic of its type, because the plot, the situation and the acting are wonderful. York and Agutter are excellent as the two leads, both finding new things about life, love and their preconceptions as the movie progresses….It has to be seen within the context of when it was made, but still worth the effort to catch.'
(Ref: http://70s.fast-rewind.com)

'The elaborate production seems typical of many sci-fi films, with artificial sets that look as if they were borrowed from Disneyland.'
(Ref: The Futura Illustrated Film Guide)

'Jenny Agutter is a wonderfully waifish Jessica 6; her character tirelessly plods after Logan, whining only occasionally about being tired or scared. Despite the fact that the film drags horribly in the

opposite: the 1976 Bantam books tie-in novel tie-in film paperback.

final forty minutes, the ending is remarkable in that it's actually subtle. There are no lengthy explanations or intrusive voice-overs, merely a wordless scene with some heartfelt acting. Kudos to director Michael Anderson for saving this movie at the last moment.'
(Ref: Chris Holland & Scott Hamilton / www.stomptokyo.com)
'Despite some dreary bits, Logan's Run isn't bad sci-fi and is an interesting exercise in what the future was thought to be like back in the 1970s: all high-tech and sanitized with clean and efficient energy, not the grungy dystopian futures depicted in films of the 1980s like Blade Runner (1982) and its ilk. Back then people still believed in a glitzier and better future.'
(Ref: James O'Ehley, members.tripod.com/scifimoviepage/)

Equus (1977) 138 mins
'Sidney Lumet was fantastic to work with, but he'd been an actor. He knew exactly what you wanted, always. He kept on piling on ideas all the time.'
Jenny interview, The Guardian, February 2002.
This is an extraordinary piece of writing and acting by playwright Peter Schaeffer and its cast members. From Richard Burton and a young Peter Firth in the leads to Colin Blakely and Joan Plowright (as the boy's parents) and a memorable Eileen Atkins in supporting roles: the casting is spot on. Jenny would play the Atkins part of as

Hesther, in the 2007 London stage revival.
Here she has another 'And Jenny Agutter' credit as a nubile young woman called Jill Mason and features briefly in 2 scenes woven into the effective trailer for this absorbing movie. Lumet, an American-born director is still making pictures in 2009 and will hopefully be adding to his eclectic CV that includes classics such as Serpico (1973), Dog Day Afternoon (1975) and Network (1976). As Jenny's opening quote clarifies, this energetic director was a great team player and worked closely with Schaeffer to bring his screenplay to life. The cast was gathered for a little over a week of rehearsal time prior to a total of 37 days filming. Such was Lumet's effectiveness; the project was finished 2 days ahead of schedule. Supposedly set in Sussex, Equus was actually filmed on location in a small town in Ontario, Canada, called Georgetown. Not that this affects the story one jot. Peter Firth plays 17-year-old Alan, whose case is referred to Dr Martin Dysart (Burton) as being one involving 'extremity.' What that actually is, proves to be the point of the film as Burton's character talks directly to camera and reveals the events that led up to the maiming of a number of horses by the youngster. The animals are stabled at a property owned by Dalton (an excellent Harry Andrews); uncle to Jill (Jenny) who exercises the horses daily. It is she who invites the curly-haired lad in to accepting a job offered by her uncle as a stable boy.

This was one of a number of weighty 1970s roles for Welsh hell-raiser Burton which also included two films both released in 1978: The Medusa Touch and Absolution. He is mesmeric as the psychiatrist whose daily chats with Alan makes him question his own unhappiness just as intensely as this troubled young man.

Lumet recreates the profound childhood experience of a 6-year-old Alan (played by an adult Firth but so creatively shot that you really believe what you see) and his life changing moment of meeting a horseman and his stead on a beach had upon him. It all sounds quite preposterous but Schaffer's screenplay, adapted virtually intact from his own provocative play, proves rewarding if a little overtly flowery in its use of language (especially by Burton in one of his many soliloquies or when talking with the lad.)

There is a whole other subtext in Equus (meaning horse from its Latin origin) it being something that the boy worships and the stable being his 'temple' and so forth. As the psychiatrist delves deeper into the psyche of his patient, they develop an intense relationship via the daily talking therapy with the 'nosey parker' doctor as Alan terms him. Firth is outstanding in his performance and quite believable throughout. There are many intensely shaded close-ups of Burton as he tells the story and it is convincing enough to the audience when he begins questioning his own life and passions via the direct simplicity of the provocative teenager.

'Tell me about Jill,' he asks as the film moves closer to revealing how his patient arrived at such a brutal act outlined above. Jenny is all jodhpurs and sex appeal here as a sexpot, slightly older woman quite bored with life and quick to make her carnal interest in Alan transparent. Although her reasoning is pretty uncomplimentary, if it was not him it would clearly be anybody else. They agree to go out, with her idea of fun being to see a Swedish adult film at the local cinema. Things go from bad to worse as Alan's uptight father (Colin Blakeley) walks into the auditorium not realizing that his son is there. Acute embarrassment ensues and his lad is ordered to leave and return home without Jenny in tow. Alan refuses and the two end up back at the stables where you may be able to imagine what happens next. The script has Firth recounting these moments sometime after they have occurred.

'Her face was so warm.' Upstairs at the stables, the slightly-built youngster knows what is about to happen but goes along in spite of his anxieties. The future Heartbeat/ And the Beat Goes On/ Spooks co-stars appear completely naked and the event proves the catalyst to Alan's complete psychological collapse. 'Are you alright?' asks the beautiful Jill, sensing his unease. 'You look weird.' It is an intense moment and you see how slight of frame the actor once was and how, well, pert Jenny was. Their brief moments on screen together are quite effective and as Jill, Jenny broaches the idea of the sexualisation/ fetishing of the horse/ stable environment (all those saddles, bits etc) to a non-committal response from Alan whom the audience knows all about by then.

As the truth of the events immediately precipitating their aborted love-making is described to the doctor, the power of the story proves exhaustive but hugely rewarding viewing. Jenny is only seen a few times and it is very much a sexualized role.

Released theatrically in October 1977 under a restricted 'AA' certification Equus did not primarily produce good box office returns. That same month Jenny along with Richard Burton appeared on the Dinah Shore television chat show in the U.S.

Burton had acted in a stage version of Equus in February 1976 for a very successful run in New York after he had agreed to appear in the forthcoming film prior to accepting the stage part as Dysart. The role had been played previously by Anthony Perkins and Anthony Hopkins (with Peter Firth involved too as well as in the original 1973 production at the National Theatre). The finished film was critically well-received and recognized by the industry with an Oscar nomination for both Burton and Finch a s well as Schaeffer's screenplay. Both actors had won Golden Globes aka 'Emmys' and Jenny was awarded a Best Supporting Actress Bafta, as indeed was the commercially-released soundtrack by Richard

Rodney Bennett. British Bafta nominations were also heralded to Schaeffer and co-stars Colin Blakeley & Joan Plowright.

Critical comments:

'…loses much of its emotional impact and imagination in the transfer from stage to screen. The performances, however, are excellent.'
(Ref: The Futura Illustrated Film Guide)

'Less effective on screen, which goes for realism and leaves little for the imagination.'
(Ref: 1000 Best movies on Video)

'For sheer mental and physical exercise, the film is an exhilarating experience.'
(Ref: Alexander Walker, Evening Standard, 1977)

'The acting throughout is of consistently high quality…while Agutter as the stable girl whose sexual advances brought about disaster for once seems to contribute some credibility to a role.'
(Ref: Tom Hutchinson, Sunday Telegraph, 23 October 1977)

'Not a great deal is seen of Jenny Agutter until she strips for the seduction scene. Any chap who prefers horses to Miss Agutter's charms would have to be mad.'
(Ref: Arthur Thirkell, Mirror, 21 October 1977)

'Two and a quarter hours is too long. The treatment is literal where it should be suggestive. The religious symbolism and pagan talk of horse fetishes sounds bogus. This is a film of quality and integrity; but as a work of art it is flawed.'
(Ref: Felix Barker, Ev. News, 20 October 1977)

The Man in the Iron Mask (1977) 101 mins

'At last producers are treating me as a grown-up. But I still feel I've got to play a really daring female role before I finally rid myself of that gymslip and white socks image!'

Jenny speaking during the production of The Man in the Iron Mask.

When this originally made-for-TV feature was awarded a cinematic release it must have pleased its first-time director Mike Newell no end. Nowadays he is a an old-hand in the film industry after helming features such as Dance with a Stranger (1985) and Four Weddings and a Funeral (1994) but back in the 1970s he was known only for his television work. Ian Holm, a supporting cast member in the film, later to find fame and much popularity in such delights as Time Bandits (1981) and Brazil (1985) spoke fondly of him. 'He had a refreshing lack of self-importance and pomposity, and not much tolerance for those who were bumptious or strutting.'

The Man in the Iron Mask, previously made as a film in 1939, was produced for Sir Lew Grade's ITC company across a six week shoot, one month being location filming in France during the hottest summer for years. Unfortunately for the cast, the film was a costume piece (for which its designer Olga Lehman was Emmy-nominated) and proved hard work in such high temperatures.

For this screen of the Alexander Dumas Pere novel set in the opulent court of Louis XIV, Jenny plays the golden locked delight that is Louise, incorporating a slightly breathy voice and looking luscious in puffy-sleeved dresses, pearls and ringlet hair. A dashing but colourless Richard Chamberlain is cast in dual roles of the pampered king and his exiled, twin brother, Philippe. The latter having no notion of his true heritage until he is discovered languishing in the bastille where Jenny's father is also held captive. It is here that Philipe's physical likeness to the King is recognized by all: including the dastardly Patrick McGoohan and separate plotters headed by a bird-like Ralph Richardson. A mute point here, but for a story set in France, no one apart from Ian Holm seems to have any intonation acknowledging the setting. McGoohan, forever regaled for his roles in The Prisoner and Danger Man, has a ball as a suitably plumy-voiced plotter whose part in the final denouement seals the reason why you should endure the film which is a little dull. He and the majestic Richardson are excellent with Holm (later to appear in The King of the Wind with Jenny) flitting in and out as various plots run parallel to depose the monarch are set in motion. After spurning the advances of Mr. McGoohan, Jenny is forced to encourage the

amorous advances of the wretched King (even though he is already married) for fear of further reprisals against her imprisoned father. It is at the prison that she first sees the 'good' Chamberlain who becomes firm friends with her fragile father. To complicate matters, the youngsters soon fall for each other. Chamberlain, now a seasoned musical theatre actor in the States, provides a great deal of swash in his buckle after previously starring in another Dumas telly adaptation, The Count of Monte Cristo (1976). And he was also in the rip-roaring Musketeers films released in the 1970s (as were Jenny associates Michael York and Frank Finlay). Richard has a bit of the Valentino look with his pencil thin moustache and smashing O.T.T poodle wig and floppy hat much favored by the aristocracy of the day. As Philippe, he is the opposite; all dashing and cavalier-like with the noble D'Artagnan (Gigi star Louis Jordan, who had acted with him in the Count of Monte Cristo) teaching him the finer skills of swordsmanship, dancing and royal history in preparation for the coup. At this stage in the story, he is unaware of his true association before a revelation which literally transforms his life.

There is a great scene wherein the peacock-strutting King meets his brother for the first time and we get two Richard Chamberlain's on-screen for the price of one. Thankfully, it is from this point on that the film receives a much-needed adrenalin boost. It all occurs during the evening of a sumptuous ball at the court where lots of twists and turns are to take place. Poor Patrick McGoohan is duped into arresting the real King instead of the 'impostor' and the look upon his face as the truth is revealed by a devilishly-calm Richardson is brilliantly done. This is devised as first the new King dances with his Queen and she sees right through him but says nothing and then Jenny takes to the floor with him as the tale is about to close.Retribution is reaped as the nasty Richard is carted off to the very same island where he had knowingly imprisoned his brother previously. Despite all his vehement protestations, he too is encased in the iron mask to disguise his identity. A great ending for a film that is not massively exciting viewing up until then when the plot pays dividends and you have to admire the whole story.

Mildly enjoyable with a bland Richard Chamberlain and cast only restricted by wordy dialogue (oddly enough, screenplay adaptor William Best was nominated for an Emmy award), The Man in the Iron Mask is perfect bank holiday teatime viewing.

The Eagle has Landed (1977) 118 mins

'Your nose turns up. Did anyone tell you that? And when you get angry your mouth turns down at the corners.'

Liam (Donald Sutherland) to the precocious Molly (Jenny) in the film.

Michael Caine, Sutherland and Robert Duvall lead a male pack in this war film taken from a best-selling Jack Higgins novel; screenplay by Tom Mankiewicz and directed by the venerable John Sturges. Writing in his autobiography, Dallas actor Larry Hagman who has a brief role in the picture, was not enamored by his director's people skills: 'He was brusque. He barked orders like an old-fashioned movie director.'

Eagle presented Jenny with an 'also starring…' credit as the feisty, teenaged Molly Pryor, who initially comes into view as a working lass in a local village. Wherein she has an immediate effect upon the newly-arrived/ smitten, Mr. Sutherland. He affects a twee Irish accent as a mercenary IRA man supporting the German plot to kidnap the British Prime Minister, Winston Churchill. The story, after advancing some 40 minutes on is where Jenny first appears; ably riding a horse and trap and later galloping off on a saddle-less horse (although it's not her in the long-shots).

Caine stars as a principled German paratrooper leading an elite squad sent to grab our war-time leader. Sounding ominous, not even Himmler (Donald Pleasance, whose daughter would later appear in a couple of projects with Jenny) thinks it a feasible idea. However, 'In 1943, sixteen German paratroopers landed in England.'

Begins the poster blurb for the film, 'In three days they almost won the war.' Whilst the American poster had the strap line of 'The daring World War II plot that changed the course of history.' The movie poster featured a montage of the cast including Jenny wielding a shotgun that she would use so fatefully in the film.

Sturges was a workmanlike director with 44 films under his belt (Eagle being his final feature) and helmed perennial telly favourite The Great Escape as well as the Magnificent Seven & Gunfight at the O.K Corral. Oddly though, he was not involved in the editing of this film prior to its commercial release. Meanwhile Mr. Caine starred in another war film released that year, A Bridge Too Far. The Eagle has Landed was one of a succession of such pictures that seemed to prevail in the late-1960s and into the 1970s.

Back to the plot, lots of believable double-crossing

ensues and Molly (Jenny) becomes embroiled when her feelings for the Irishman prove strong enough for her to turn a shotgun on a failed suitor once the dastardly German plot is discovered. All cloak & dagger stuff and no less watchable for that, the action progresses whilst the tight-curled hair belonging to the buxom Miss Pryor disappears. Jenny returns to the story nearly two hours in wherein she, Caine & Sutherland share a brief moment on screen as the former attempt to flee the village once the scheme fails.

Many are killed in the film but these two men manage to escape only for the latter to say that he is going back to find his lover, as his feelings towards her prove all-consuming. Caine continues on alone to complete his mission and finally comes face to face with Mr. Churchill in this lengthy feature or at least he thinks he does.

Some enjoyable scenes and a strong cast also look out for a gung ho officer Larry Hagman whose fate is sealed as soon as the audience sees him.

Eagle was shot across 16 weeks over the summer months and more in locations that utilized Norfolk, Finland, Jersey and Twickenham studios. Watch out to for an interesting role for Anthony Quayle. He does not get to do very much but his association with Jenny would continue as the two had already acted in East of Sudan (1964) and would later reconvene for King of the Wild (1990). In 2007 a short documentary was released titled The Eagle has Landed Revisited: Invading Mapledurham. It showed production designer Peter Murton returning to the Berkshire village where he remembers the effect that filming had upon the place all those years ago. A number of location adaptations were made that benefited the locale including a row of fake shops built on the church car park and a nearby pub which much to the chagrin of all did not serve real beer! The watermill seen in the film is a replica after the then-owner of the Mapledurham estate, one Jack Eyston, refused permission to blow up the derelict original (since restored). Regional journalist Tom Hepworth also visited the village for his BBC South Today programme wherein Mr.Eyston commented, 'They (the film makers) had to paint the grass green by the end of that long hot summer but they left the place in a much better state than when they arrived.' The region had quite a lasting affect upon Ms.Agutter too and her fondness for the coast has since blossomed.

Critical comments:

'The picture wasn't bad, but I still get angry when I think what it could have been with the right director.' Michael Caine

'It's a film with no pretensions and director Sturges keeps things moving at a robust pace…' (Ref: Citizencaine.org - a Michael Caine fan site)

'Based on a best-selling tall story by Jack Higgins, and featuring an all-star cast that must've cost half the budget just to get to sign up for the project, The Eagle Has Landed is an enjoyable but slightly

overlong wartime actioner.
(Ref: Jonathon Dabell, Amazon.com)

China 9, Liberty 37 (1978) 102 mins
'I had a feeling you were gonna be trouble.'
Also known as 'Amore, piombo e furore' as well as
'Clayton & Catherine' aka 'Clayton Drumm' and
'Gunfire & Love, Bullets and Frenzy' for its later
American video release.
If you as a viewer manage to make it through the
first hour of this Italian-Spanish co-production,
shot in Spain and studios in Rome, you are to be
applauded. Directed by cult American creative
Monte Hellman, the film opens with a sultry
Catherine (Jenny) seen enjoying a cool down in a
river. She is subsequently overseen by a
mysterious stranger, Italian beefcake Fabio Testi
whom it transpires is looking for her much-older
husband (an ever-dependable Warren Oates who
had previously worked with Hellman) for reasons
that are already outlined onscreen.
It is clear that Catherine and Drumm (Testi) have
the hots for each other and prior to the first of his
initial departures, they make love. Although the
cuckold Matthew (Oates) insinuates that his
beautiful young wife has strayed before, she later
contradicts this view when with her lover.
Continuing in her love-ruling-her-head batch of
characters (see The Eagle has Landed or
Dominique is Dead) her character plunges a knife
into her husband to prevent him from harming the
departing Italian gun slinger. Mistakenly believing
that she has killed him, Jenny leaves to follow her
lover; but chaos soon ensues from the Jerry
Harvey-Douglas Venturelli screenplay.
'I sure made a mess of things!' wheezes an
exasperated Catherine following her enforced
return to her husband. And watching the first hour
or so does make you ponder as to why people got
involved with this project. However, after a bit of
perseverance, it is worth the ride.
Testi and Jen's characters share a tender moment
when the former reveals his past to a lover that
desperately wants them to be together. They agree
to try but have their moment interrupted soon
enough by the reappearance of her furious husband
accompanied by a belligerent posse.
In the final moments, the reunited couple and co-
horts return home only to be set upon by rogues
employed by the railroad (who want to develop the
land owned by Oates). A shoot-out ensues with a
great many killings. Thanks to the assistance of her
re-emerged lothario, the attack is successfully
fended off but only 3 survive: Jenny, Oates &
Testi. The bemused Oates thanks him for his help
and says that Catherine is free to leave although he
would prefer it if she remained with him. It is still
not over between the two men, as honour abounds
and the former demands a duel. The usurper draws
his gun first but chooses not to kill his opponent
and simply leaves his tearful lover behind.
Finally, the married couple depart together in what

shows itself to be quite a touching finale. Jenny's character has had to accept the fact that her desire for the robust Testi is just not meant to be. Sam Peckinpah, the renowned director and role model for Hellman, features briefly in what transpires to be a genuine curiosity piece.

Trinity Home Entertainment produced a DVD presentation of the film with a 92 minutes running time. However, it transpires that this version was heavily edited, not unlike the Bingo Video offering which is said to contain nude scenes of Miss Agutter. Also, screenwriting credits have offered Ennio De Concini and Alberto Liberati as additional contributors.

An example of the quirkiness seen in China 9, Liberty 37 finds Waren Oates' brother and friends pay a fleeting visit and where they take turns to sing and Jenny does her bit which sounds really awful. And none of the others seem to like it much either! Well, Jenny must have possessed some actual talent as she provided backing vocals for Prefab Sprout on their LP track 'Wild Horses' from the 1990 album Jordan: The Comeback. Released in August 1990, it made the Top 10 on the charts. Finally, if you are wondering about the significance of the film's title, it is a reference to a sign post viewed on screen early on. On the macabre front, American scriptwriter Jerry Harvey subsequently committed suicide by using a gun that had belonged to China 9 actor Sam Peckinpah.
Critical comments:

'1978 may seem a little late for a "Spaghetti Western", but as the final Western feature made by either Warren Oates or director Monte Hellman, it's definitely an important one. It's also laced with just as much meaning as Hellman's other films. This film may not have always had the greatest reputation…still, the movie rises way above its minimal budget to reach for greatness, and the result is as pure Monte Hellman as any of the director's other films. In the end there's a lot of dead bodies & eventually nobody really gets what they want.'
(Ref: Ron Wells/ www.filmthreat.com)

'I got this film for one reason. Jenny Agutter is one of the most beautiful women in the world. Anyone who disagrees should go back and see Logan's Run. Unfortunately Jenny has very little to do in this movie except look pretty, but even her great beauty is concealed most of the time. As Italian westerns go, I suppose it is passable, but without Clint Eastwood in it, who cares. There are many westerns, even Italian westerns that are much better. Unless you are as big a fan of Agutter as I am, chose Silvarado or some other much better western.'
(Ref: http://www. getcheap-movies.com)

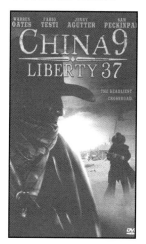

'Hellman's seriously absurdist streak happily finds a comically absurd parallel within the stereotyped framework of the European western: he revels in the sheer gratuitousness of traditional character-types and plot mechanisms to produce an uproarious genre critique.'
(Ref: PT - Time Out Film Guide, timeout.com)
'Though not without its moments this feature lacks the rigors of Hellman's other brilliant westerns, sharing the brilliance only in a tight minimalist narrative and in a created humorous absurdist world.' (Ref: Dennis Schwartz, www.sover.net)

Dominique is Dead (1978) 100 mins
'It sounds so unbelievable: pianos playing, faces in the night, bodies hanging…gravestones.'
Ann (Jenny) in the film.
Just like Ms.Agutter, Jean Simmons possesses one of the most beautiful, instantly recognizable screen faces. Starring as the lady of the title, Ms.Simmons and everyone else in this thrilling piece puts in a gripping performance. Adapted by the writing team of Edward and Valerie Abraham from an original story by Harold Lawler, they also co-wrote the story used in Murder Elite, a 1985 feature film directed by Sweet William helmer Claude Whatham. The Abrahams furnished the same duties on Monster Club (1980) which saw a role for Donald Pleasance.
Shot at Shepperton studios, this has Logan's Run director Michael Anderson orchestrating some excellent plot twists and turns (some predictable and others not so). Oscar winning American actor Cliff Robertson portrays the emotionally-detached husband to Dominique (Simmons) with a radiant Jenny Agutter as his half-sister, Ann.
Jenny does not feature greatly in the story initially, and you are left wondering if her character actually has anything to do here. However, her role proves pivotal, with all being revealed in a smashingly entertaining finale that's worth the wait.
With the adage that for every action there is a reaction; Dominique is Dead offers many suppositions that spin back on themselves and leave the audience enthralled. The characterization may be a bit sparse, especially Robertson's, but you keep watching to see how things pan out.
Jenny associate Judy Geeson, older sister of Bless This House poppet Sally, has a small role and would also briefly appear in The Eagle has Landed (she is seen also in I Start Counting). An interesting point about Ms Geeson is that after moving to the States and appearing in various small screen shows there, she did voluntary work alongside Jenny and others in Los Angeles, where they brought Shakespeare to local youngsters. Like Jenny, the young Judy wanted to be a ballerina but unlike her friend, did not attain her goal to be so.
Critical appraisal varies greatly towards this film but after viewing this directly after The Survivor, I have to say Dominique, described on its DVD release as a 'twisting tale of avenging spirits',

proves much the more entertaining of the two.
Director Anderson has since made it known that
the film was edited without his involvement and
that the character portrayed by Ron Moody had
much of his work cut out of the final print.
Released as part of a double-feature, the film was
a second picture support to Seven, an adult 'X'
adult thriller: Dominique was an 'AA' certification.
The under-rated Simon Ward continued his
working association with Jenny here after pursuing
her across a common in I Start Counting (1969).
Also known as Dominique and Avenging Spirit
with its longer title being used for its re-issue in
America & subsequent UK video release, the
movie tagline featured the line 'Dominique is dead
or is she?' Whilst its British theatrical copy line
offered, 'A story of the macabre...with a different
twist.'
When Jenny tried her luck as an actress in
Hollywood at the ripe young age of twenty-one,
she was screen tested by a certain director for a
role in an un-named film but was not successful:
the director was one Michael Anderson.
Critical comments:
'…a very parsimonious production with little to
hold the interest.'
(Ref: Leslie Halliwell, Film Guide, 6th ed)
'Moribund thriller.'
(Ref: Steven Scheuer, Movies on TV)
'Dominique's ethereal air is well sustained by Jean
Simmons whom it is good to see back on the

screen again. Jenny Agutter isn't all she seems to
be though she covers it up very cleverly.'
(Ref: Un-credited film magazine article)

The Riddle of the Sands (1979) 99 mins.
'In these shifting sands, men can disappear without
a trace…and their secrets with them.' Film tagline
Based upon the elongated 1903 espionage novel
by Erskine Childers, significant in that it is
regarded as being the precursor to the advent of
the spy novel, The Riddle of the Sands passes the
time admirably. Although, it does feel all a bit
Boy's Own (with lots of 'I say!' heralding in its
plotting and characterization). As Clara, Jenny's
character floats in and out of the story and simply
appears and disappears.
Set around a German island of key strategic
significance, leading cast members Simon
MacCorkindale and a dapper Michael York play

former Oxford chums reunited over a secret plot to invade England. Led by the Kaiser himself (as portrayed by German character man Wolf Kahler, who made an un-credited apperance in Jenny's The Eagle has Landed) there is a great deal of derring-do going on.

Jenny looks lovely with chest-length hair, beautifully dressed in period clothes consisting of long skirts, straw hat and at times, a beret. It is little wonder that Davies (the dashing MacCorkindale) immediately becomes smitten by the affluent young German girl. Still acting in the theatre and on television, Simon gained success in America on the soap opera Falcon Crest prior to more recently featuring in a mass of episodes of medical series Casualty. Like Jenny, he has also acted in Shakespearian productions.

Back to the book, a best-seller which has dated but back when it was published it did strike a chord with its readership in outlining the risk held by Germany during that period. Britain had recently been un-successfully involved in the Boer War and many in the country feared outsiders. The Riddle of the Sands proved to be the only screenplay adaptation from John Bailey (of which he co-wrote with director Tony Maylam). Utilising locations in Holland, the Frisian Islands in the former West Germany and Hertfordshire studios in the UK, Sands is a jolly wheeze with a great soundtrack accompaniment from The Snowman composer Howard Blake. Not only that, it looks fabulous and a big thumbs up to director of photography, Christopher Challis.

It is Davies who falls for Clara (Jenny) and she even has some brief lines of German dialogue as the daughter of Dollman, double-agent Alan Badel in one of the 'baddy' roles. But it is still great to see the Logan's Run duo of York/ Agutter back together on screen even though they share only brief moments. York and MacCorkindale prove a decent screen team and primarily it is the latter that commands much of the film up until the arrival of the spoilt 'toff' Carruthers. Michael provides the voice-over narration and both actors work well-together. Love fortunately does conquer all for Jenny and Simon as along with his pal, they return safely to England to relay plans of the

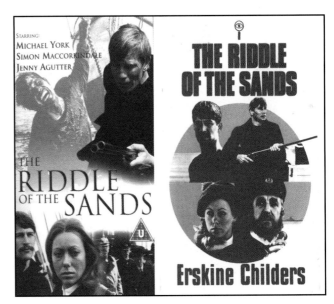

thwarted German attack to those that need to know. Jenny's character having no insight into her deceitful father's involvement with the Germans (his identity is not as it initially seems) agrees to stay with her love whilst her father and step-mother become fatalities via an attack by a pursuing German naval boat looking for the two Englanders.

Watch out for a rigorous performance from Michael Sheard as one of the plotters. Some viewers will remember him as the evil Mr.Bronson in Grange Hill. He and The Survivor man Robert Powell later worked together on TV's Hannay. Sheard acted in many other projects including Danger:UXB with Jenny co-star Judy Geeson. The Riddle of the Sands was re-made for German television in 1987 as Das Rätsel der Sandbank, a longer version closer to the book than the film, which juxtaposed the order of the story. The real-life of author, sailor and writer Childers concluded with his execution via a firing squad during the Irish civil war. He had put his nautical skills to good use for Britain in World War I, but later became embroiled with the Irish rebels who opposed the Anglo-Irish Treaty; the outcome of which saw the 1922 formation of the Free State and partition.

The Riddle of the Sands, a million pound production, marked its first day of shooting in April '78 although bizarrely enough in the world of cinema where artifice rules, a key scene was actually shot in London (where the 2 male leads get caught in fog).

Childer's publishers insisted that Jenny's character be included in the film screenplay which seems an odd request but York felt it was a good idea to stop the film becoming a boy's own type adventure (although I have to say that this failed). Michael had previously been involved in attempting to adapt the book into a film and as he mentions in his autobiography, he still wants to make a biography feature about Childers life.

Critical comments:

'Nothing suggests 1970s and 1980s cheese quite like the triumvirate of Michael York, Simon MacCorkindale and Jenny Agutter.
(Ref: Richard Luck, channel4.com)

'The predictable action unfolds unconvincingly, taking place mostly at sea. Settings tend to be lavish, and the main riddle here is why so much money and effort were expended to prop up a weak script.'
(Ref: Futura Illustrated Film Guide)

'No one has ever done a better job of transferring this lesser-known classic story to the screen. York, MacCorkindale and Agutter are seldom better than they are here in quiet and understated performances. The director achieves the very spirit of the book in a seemingly effortless manner.'
(Ref: beeryusa, Imdb.co.uk)

'The film version is a slow but affable period piece…appearances tend to upstage everything

else about the film; Agutter may stumble somewhat with the German accent required by the story (she calls Arthur "Arsa"), but she looks great… Mr. York fortunately makes fun of his own stuffiness…and…becomes a suitably vigorous leading man. Mr. MacCorkindale grows more plausible as the spy story progresses. But he has such a slow, wide-eyed delivery at first that he appears to be addressing himself to the grade-school set, which may indeed constitute the film's ideal audience.'
(Ref: Janet Maslin, http://movies.nytimes.com)
'…perfectly civilized and satisfying low-key adventure film.'
(Ref: Steven H.Scheuer - Movies on TV and videocassette guide)
'Muted version of Childers' classic spy story that looks the part but fails to set the pulses racing.'
(Ref: 1000 Best movies on Video)

Sweet William (1980) 92 mins
'A wonderful part. Really terrific to have something to get one's teeth into.
A charming film, a very fun book and good film.'
Jenny speaking about the film some years later of her role as Ann.
Released in cinemas back in April 1980 Sweet William began its life as a 1975 novel by Liverpool-born author Beryl Bainbridge.
Ms.Bainbridge adapted her work into her first feature film screenplay which was directed by

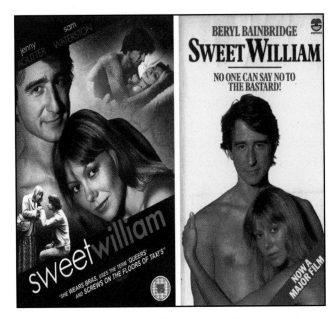

Claude Whatham. His film / portfolio concluding with the 1991 feature Buddy's Song before his death in 2008.
When Ann's boyfriend departs alone for a job in America he leaves her behind with the promise of sending for her at a later stage. Big mistake as the duplicitous William (Sam Waterson) commences his courtship of her in such a whirlwind manner that before you know it, they are in bed together.
Costumed in a long skirt and tweed jacket (elements of which are all in the novel which saw a reprint when the film was released) her appearance contrasts abruptly with the scruffiness of the denim-clad William.
Waterson portrays a cocky, dislikeable cad that somehow manages to seduce Ann as well as many

others across the city. In amongst some grating dialogue there are occasional gems; 'You don't seem to understand,' offers a perturbed Jenny after yet another revelation, 'it's the number of wives that causes the confusion!' The character of the American playwright comes across as even more disagreeable in the novel and watching the film I too had the feeling that the actors showed very little chemistry (or is it their characters that irk and thus work as intended?)

The story becomes very silly and overwrought for all the women in the compartmentalized life of the American and clearly something has to give. Indeed it does when Ann falls pregnant but still William refuses or is unable to change his philandering ways. It has to be acknowledged that he never actually lies; simply that he does not explain his associations fully to her. When he does it proves quite a bombshell for a bemused Ann. Waterson is mainly known today for his long-running role in hit American telly series Law & Order. Acting in films since the 1960s as well as theatre, he is remembered for The Killing Fields (1984) and in some Woody Allen pictures. Also in amongst a strong cast is the marvelous Arthur Lowe, part of the National Theatre production of The Tempest, along with Jenny in 1974. Here he portrays her father, a deeply troubled man of few words whose presence remains with the viewer long after the memory of the film begins to fade. Remembered by children of a certain age as the voice of the Mr. Men, he came to acting professionally aged 30 and enjoyed a fruitful career from then on. Co-star Malcolm McDowell credited him as 'the best character actor you could ever possibly work with.' The super Anna Massey is also in the film and would repeat her working association with Jenny some years later on televison in A Respectable Trade.

There is a neat twist at the close of the story appertaining to the birth of Jenny's screen baby (just as William does another disappearing act). However, neither she nor her beau, are characters that the audience particularly warms to. So in all, quite an odd little feature.

Critical comments:

'Instead of feeling any sense of identification with the lovers in this 'contemporary romance', the sheer implausibility of their relationship leads to an intense sense of frustration and confusion as to which of the two one would most like to strangle.' (Ref: author FF, Time Out Film Guide)

'Not nearly as hip or contemporary as it apparently imagines itself to be, Whatham's film suffers from a complete lack of chemistry between its two leads. Made a coupe of years after punk had hit town, it must have seemed very old-fashioned even when it was first released.' (Ref: Channel4.com)

'Despite the presence of a decent cast, this portrait of a rather unpleasant cad lacks a real cutting edge. (Ref: Radio Times Guide to Films 2007)

'Agutter is well-cast, and good in that her seduction by the outlandish Waterston is entirely believable.' (Ref: Variety Movie Guide 1999)

An American Werewolf in London (1981)
95 mins

'She's just so stunning.'
Co-star Griffin Dunne speaking about Jenny on a DVD commentary of An American Werewolf in London.
Next to The Railway Children and Logan's Run, this is one of the defining films that people recognize Jenny Agutter for being in. Some may hold fond memories of a bubbly Barbara Windsor squashed into a nurse's uniform in a couple of the saucy 'Carry On' films but for others, the image of

an incandescent Jenny as nurse Alex in An American Werewolf in London is all-pervasive.
Writer-director and sometime hammy-actor John Landis created an original screenplay back in 1969 but would not obtain funding to make his feature until more than a decade later. He did not have his actors rehearse

much before shooting but was prone to distributing detailed background hand-outs prior to filming. Made across February - March 1981, the finished film, shot in sequence and under serious secrecy, was made available for theatrical release that same August. Landis has since stated that although the film is played straight it also has a bucket full of droll (and often un-subtle) black humour coursing through it which confounded the critics who sought to categorize it. Making the most of a modest budget of a $1m much of which was spent on the ground-breaking and award-winning special effects by Rick Baker, London was the third horror feature of the early-1980s. It followed on from two other 1981 presentations: The Howling and Wolfen. A continuation of the theme returned in 1997 with the cinema release of An American Werewolf in Paris; although minus Jenny.

The film has a number of character parts for up-and-coming British faces such as comedy man Rik Mayal and a scene-stealing Brian Glover. Although the latter, a former wrestler, does not appear on screen with Jenny he proves a memorable presence as a twitchy local advising the 2 male Americans to stay off the moors…Also seen at the Slaughtered Lamb public house, utilized early on in the story and prior to the attack of the tourists, Lila Kaye features as the bar maid. She would go on to act directly alongside Jenny in an episode of the terrible Dear John: USA television series in 1989 but doesn't share any screen time with her here.

The pub seen in the film was actually a private residency mocked-up. John Woodvine is memorable too as a doctor working at the same hospital as Nurse Jenny in caring for the traumatized David (David Naughton) following the fateful attack resulting in the grizzly death of his companion Griffin Dunne. The role of the former, according to future director Dunne, was originally penciled in for Jenny's September screen husband James Fox. Dunne, an under-used actor starred in such delights as After Hours (1985) features in a segment of Amazon Woman on the Moon (1987) which included a separate cameo from Jenny.

The-then 30 year-old Naughton, who's CV has not amounted to much since this, is cast as the soul-survivor of a werewolf attack on a desolate moor (actually filmed in Windsor Park and Hay Bluff, on the Brecon Beacons, Wales).

Jenny arrives on screen a little over a quarter-hour in. She is cast as Nurse Alex Price, pristine in a white, pressed uniform resplendent with hat (no longer worn nowadays due to cleanliness reasons) and the trusty upside-down watch with curls spilling out of her hat. As the injuries sustained by David necessitate him staying in hospital for a few days, he has individual care provided by Nurse Jenny; and who would want to leave? The fictitious hospital where she offers David extra-special care, has to be the only NHS facility where you see the same nurse twice let alone have

stories read to you (as he does here). As the plot unravels, David begins to have horrific nightmares and in one Jenny is hacked to death with loads of exaggerated blood all over the place. In spite of the handsome young American saying he sees dead people and is going to turn into a werewolf, his dedicated carer invites him to stay with her after he is released.

They return to her rather spacious flat in Knightsbridge (it can be located in Redcliffe Square, near Earl's Court in S.W.10) and get better acquainted. It is here that the two become lovers and snog in the shower to the ironic strains of Van Morrison's 'Moondance' before engaging in a full-on bout of shagging thereafter! Some interior shots were filmed in a mock-up of the flat back at Twickenham studios.

Things are soon spoilt as his 'undead' buddy Dunne appears and freaks his pal out. A very dark-haired Jenny looks highly attractive in the film but you do have to wonder just what she sees in this dull, Stateside visitor. Landis had seen Naughton in a soft drinks commercial and subsequently cast him in the role of David. His career never really took off after this but the cult film that Werewolf now is means that he is forever associated with it. Not a big hit upon its release, its status as a cult title blossomed from its original video release.

A half-dozen murders are committed with David proving responsible and that's why Dunne and all the victims encourage him to kill himself before he inflicts further pain in the midst of his 'carnivorous lunar activities'. All this occurs inside a sex cinema off Piccadilly Circus in the heart of London's glamorous West End.

As the story reaches its sad end, Ann (Jenny) pleads with her werewolf lover whilst he is trapped by armed police in an alleyway, 'David, please let me help you!' Alas, they shoot and his appearance returns to that of a man.

A documentary featuring Jenny titled 'Beware the Moon: Remembering An American Werewolf in London' was released in 2008 with the Blu ray version of the film being made available for the first time in that format in 2009. She is also interviewed in the small-screen documentary The Perfect Scary Movie (2005) which also saw contributions from John Landis and horror writer James Herbert (whose book 'The Survivor' was made in to a film which Jenny starred in). As well as in the excellent telly documentary 'British Film Forever (2007).

Critical comments:
'A clever mixture of comedy and horror that succeeds in being both funny and scary.'
(Ref: Variety Movie Guide 1999).
'Funny and scary' Actor Griffin Dunne.
'It's weird. It's not a very good film.'
(Ref: Roger Ebert's Movie Home Companion 1990)

Amy (1981) 100 mins

'She taught them to speak. They taught her to love.' Film poster blurb.

Made by Walt Disney Productions Amy or Amy on the Lips as it was known for its one hour version sent out to educational establishments (the longer title refers to the sign language recognition of her name and the working tile of the finished film).

Set in the America of the mid-1930s, it is not the most dynamic of stories but it proves amiable enough viewing and Jenny looks well-suited to its lovely period setting. Again she wears lots of puffed-sleeved blouses and soft pastel colours as Amy Medford, the estranged wife of a man who treats her as his possession and blames her inadequacies for the death of their young child.

Written by debutant screenwriter Noreen Stone and directed by Vincent McEveety, the film begins with our heroine seen leaving the marital home and symbolically taking her wedding ring off and placing it on the table. She leaves Boston to take up a job teaching speech at a school for the deaf (they also have blind pupils too) with an accent that has a tendency to fluctuate at the end of sentences. The then-29 year-old actress is recognizably Jenny but on occasions sounds Irish/ Australian and correctly, mid-American.

Amy teaches at a school where very little is expected of the pupils and at which few hold any positive belief that she will succeed. A lot of things go on during the course of the story and Jenny's character becomes very close to the children, especially Henry (played by a smashing Otto Rechenberg in his only acting role). Set in a period where disabilities such as blindness and deafness meant that through ignorance many were uncertain how to deal with these youngsters, who were simply kept away from everyday folk. Amy (Jenny) lives at the school and soon catches the eye of the local doctor, Ben Corcoran, played by Barry Newman. As the two become closer, the tragedy of losing her own child some 3 years before, also deaf, weighs heavily in her heart and being around the children at the school proves a challenge for her in many, many ways.

'Life here is hard,' offers the manager at the school, 'I told you that.' This coming after the accidental death of a young man there which causes Amy to feel that things are all too much for her. In the midst of falling in love with Ben (Newman) Amy is pursued by a private detective employed by her estranged husband (a suitably dull Chris Robinson) who eventually traces her whereabouts. She refuses to go back to her old subservient life and recognizes that the youngsters have also helped her come to terms with her grief and enhance her self-confidence whilst she assists them in their speech skills development.

The story is not all downbeat; Jenny looks smashing throughout wearing her hair scrunched up into a bun and in one scene even joining in with the youngsters in a game of American football!

Working on Amy found Jenny back under the Disney umbrella nearly two decades since acting in their TV feature Ballerina in 1966. Amy was released within the Walt Disney Productions/Buena Vista label. Its subsequent VHS release was under the Walt Disney Home Video banner.

The opening and closing theme song 'So many ways' sung by Julie Budd proves memorable too. Many of the children in the supporting cast were from the California School for the Deaf.

Critical comments: 'Neither preachy nor sentimental: ideal family fare.'
(Ref: Steven H.Scheuer, Movies on TV, 1989-90)

The Survivor (1981) 83 mins

'A tale of death, and of an evil which transcends death.' Prism Leisure DVD tagline.

Other video cover tag lines included: 'There was one survivor - but was he really alive!' & 'Pilot error or supernatural terror? Only 1 man can tell!'

Shot in southern Australia during spring 1980 and at that region's corporation studios, The Survivor became the first antipodean film to cost more than $1m [Australian] to make. The country had recently introduced tax incentives to shoot 'down under' and so the film was made there for that very reason. It had begun its life as a 1976 James Herbert novel and despite its failure at the box office proved to be the first of his 4 books transferred to the screen. Herbert, a huge name in the supernatural/horror genre, would see his printed work adapted by David Ambrose and directed by 1960s acting icon David Hemmings. The latter would later act on screen with Jenny's The Eagle had Landed co-star, Michael Caine, in Last Orders(1991). Blow Up (1966) had made the former a star after he had been performing since a teenager and by the 1980s he was directing such U.S. television shows as The A-Team and Magnum P.I (a separate episode of which Jenny appeared in). Ambrose had previously written an episode of the cult 1970s series Public Eye. Herbert had no contact with the film-makers prior to production and stated publicly his frustration and anger with the finished project. His book had initially been optioned by one of the Hollywood studios and could have sold for a lot more money than it did. Biographer Craig Cabell mentions that Herbert fell asleep when seeing the film at a screening!

'A supernatural story and it isn't clear whether the crash has actually happened or has yet to be.' So offered Jenny to journalist Iain F. Mc Ash about a role for which she received second-billing to Robert Powell it's a film which begins strongly but proves ultimately to be a disappointment. Leading man Powell had worked with Survivor director Hemmings the previous year on Harlequin (1980) and with Ms Agutter as the married couple in the BBC play Shelley (1972). Back in uniform once again after similar shenanigans in Tommy (1975) Powell plays Keller, a pilot who is the only survivor of a plane crash which kills more than 300 passengers on board. This supernatural tale opens eerily with the appearance of Jenny and a group of children as the aviation disaster takes place above. The Survivor is an un-nerving psychological trip with Jenny portraying Hobbs, someone that telly psychic Derek Acorah would today term as a 'sensitive' i.e. someone who is in contact with the dead. 'They're asking for your help.' Offers Jenny at one stage to a perplexed Keller.

The leads play well enough as they come together to try to piece the events of what happened after she is visited by her 'chattering friends' in need of help. When violent incidents begin to affect those involved with the tragedy and its aftermath, be it a photographer and his assistant, a police detective or doctor, Jenny's association with the troubled pilot is to prove fateful.

Regrettably, the film was severely re-edited after completion by its producer and of course, there are lots of holes in the plot and not all are clearly explained, this is especially true following the restaging of the accident by Robert and Jenny within the remnants of the burnt-out cockpit. The plot becomes confusing as its chronology blurs and the opening scene featuring Jenny and the children is repeated with additional involvement from Powell only seen in a small bi-plane rather than charter.

The Survivor is eerie stuff and watching the events unfold you really do not want a visit from the young girl whose appearance on screen signifies great danger. Re-watching the film on DVD, the perception of Hobbs (Jenny) and her manipulation by the perished voices, changes. She says to Keller (Powell) that they need his help but although he wants to know what happened and why he alone survived, the end results will not be beneficial to his well-being.

Where the film fails is in its final denouement which proves such an anti-climax after all that has transpired that it leaves the viewer feeling deflated. It is preceded by some very facile and pretentious language when the reason d'être is revealed but proves underwhelming.

Seen briefly as an un-named priest, The Survivor recorded the final film appearance by veteran Hollywood actor Joseph Cotton (of The Third Man fame). Also, Jenny who appears very pretty on screen with her hair in a bun, bits dangling either side of her face looks really attractive. She is seen immediately as the film commences and although quite beautiful looking she has quite a bit of make-up on. In addition, her performance was nominated for the Best Actress in a Lead role by the Australian Film Institute in 1981.

Jenny went off to America straight after making this picture across its 6-week shoot to try her luck in tinsel town where she would remain for the next 15 years or so.

Critical comments:

'It's as if the film had bits of its story missing and indeed the film was cut by Gianne[the producer because he felt that Hemming's direction was too "lugubrious". Whether it ever made any sense we may never know but certainly in its day it was cold-shouldered by local critics and public-alike although apparently finding popularity in France…'
(Ref: Cinephilia.net.au)

'Despite the eerie mood and a fascinating concept, Hemmings oddity fails to build any tension or realize the films potential.'
(Ref: Britmovie.co.uk)

'I thought Survivor had some extraordinary qualities to it, marred a little by the version that Tony [the producer] ultimately released was a straight forward horror film. We had originally decided we were making more of a psychological

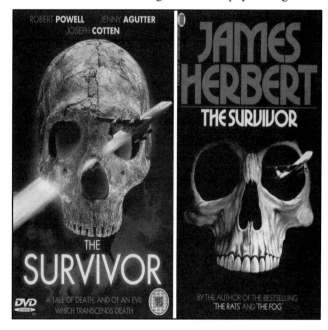

thriller…where the horror was intellectual rather than axe in your face.'
Director David Hemmings writing in his autobiography (see bibliography).

Donna giusta, La (1982) 87 mins

Aka Miss Right for its US release, Jenny has an uncredited cameo as a victim of a purse snatcher! Leading females in the cast were Margot Kidder and Karen Black whilst its male lead William Tepper does not seemed to have appeared in films since the 1980s.
With Paul Williams, who wrote & directed the film (and has a cameo) both created the story from which a screenplay was written by Tepper alone. Shot in Italy in 1980 the film failed to get a theatrical release in America but was subsequently released on video with a number of cuts: a victim of which was Jenny who only appears in the opening minute.
The basic plot premise being a Rome-based man in search of his ideal woman but failing miserably in attaining 'Miss Right'.
Critical comments:
'The actors are wasted in this tripe of an unfunny slapstick of sorts comedy that look's quite dated.' (Ref: Adrian Kiaser / Amazon.com)

Secret Places (1984) 97 minutes.

'Sometimes the heart is the most secret place of all.' Film poster strapline.

Set in the early-1940s within the closed confines of a girls day school, Secret Places focuses on the arrival of a German refugee family in amongst a twitchy town. Much suspicion and fear grows as the war progresses and the family suffer greatly as a consequence.
Laura (the debuting Marie-Theres Relin) is the young newcomer befriended by Patience (Tara MacGowran) and the two soon become close friends in this perfectly well-executed film from writer/ director Zelda Barron. Its primary source being taken from the 1962 book by the journalist and novelist Janice Elliott. She also had another of her novels; The Buttercup Chain made into a film back in 1970.
Dear Jenny is fourth-billed as the likeable English mistress Miss Lowrie in what was a six-week film shoot. She features in a few scenes but the emphasis of the story is on the dynamics of the relationship between the school friends and their associates. Much drama ensues with suicide attempts, teenage pregnancy, first love and a whole lot more. Relin & MacGowran both come from acting families of some pedigree and are watchable

as the two leads as are a number of the supports, especially Cassie Stuart as Rose. Most of the actors are too mature for their parts but it does not detract from the effectiveness of the story.

Not the least bit cinematic except for one scene it settles upon developing the characters inner-relationships in a very pedestrian manner.

I think that Jenny always lends herself well to period piece films/ drama and here is a typical example. She looks quite lovely with a mightily-stacked hair style nestling atop of her head. Also when Miss Lowrie organises a theatre production of The Three Sisters, one of the lads catches her under the mistletoe and enjoys quite a long snog with her! Indeed, the first time we see Jenny, she is reciting Keats to her class during a lesson and her dulcet tones are again maximised when the girls see young soldiers marching outside the school as the war comes ever closer to them.

The 'secret places' of the title is a reference to the various locations where the pubescent girls meet. Laura and Patience see their blossoming relationship momentarily usurped by the arrival of a young chap that both have feelings for. Although really what they both seek is to explore the idea of being in a generic emotional relationship be it with a boy or girl as both are willingly open young women keen to experience life and all its travails. The German-born Ms.Relin still acts but Ms.MacGowran is no longer doing so. Barron went on to direct a trio of Culture Club pop

promos and further films. She died in 2006.

Secret Places was the first film project invested in by Richard Branson and his Virgin company as part of an unsuccessful investment scheme.

Critical comments:

'...a complex, intelligent, beautiful film....[The] performances and the wealth of emotional detail that suffuses the film mark a first-rate debut...'
(Ref: Sheila Benson - Los Angeles Times)

'The delicate blossoming of the teenager's friendship…could have made an impactful film if the director had a firmer grasp on the best way to tell this story.'
(Ref: Steven H.Scheuer, Movies on TV, 1989-90)

'…a pleasing evocation of schoolgirl life in England during WWII.'
(Ref: Variety Movie Guide)

'Beautifully acted and sensitively written & directed, I recommend it highly.'
(Ref: Alan Frank, Daily Star)

'…so full of life and intelligence…'
(Ref: Linda Blandford, Guardian, 8 May 1985)

'A warm, realistic, unsentimental film with a fine cast…'
(Ref: Ian Christie, Daily Express, 1984.)

'From time-to-time the British film industry comes up with a gem. Secret Places is the genuine article.'
(Ref: Arthur Thirknell, Daily Mirror, 4 May 1984)

Dark Tower (1987) 91 mins

'In a city that never sleeps…This building is a nightmare.' Poster strap line.

I was quite uncertain as to what to make of this late-1980s psychological horror from director Ken Barnett. Did he specifically request that his actors, including Jenny Agutter, to mercilessly 'ham' it up in this by-the-numbers genre film making? A blaring, sub-standard Jon Michel Jarre synth-laden soundtrack does not enhance proceedings either but when it is used more subtly, the results prove palatable in enhancing the shock levels.

Shot on location in Spain for no apparent reason, Dark Tower is the skyscraper designed by the glamorous and recently-widowed architect Carolyn Page (Jenny). A workaholic, she looks stunning with lovely naval-length hair, a little too much make-up and faux American accent. Jenny appears immaculately dressed and shows herself as an all-grown-up, previously glimpsed as a blossoming beauty in A War of Children (1972). Some inept dialogue is spouted throughout and top-billed Michael Moriarty puts in an asinine performance only pepping up once the murdered spirit of Carolyn's husband attempts to communicate his anger through him. The tall American actor had previously worked with Jenny's Sweet William (1980) co-star Sam Waterson and coincidentally, was replaced by Sam in the popular Law & Order telly series.

'There's something screwy here!' Spouts Randall (Moriarty) as he begins his internal investigation in the building and it is clear from their first meeting that Jenny and Randall share a mutual attraction (although I would have to say that her character seems sexually-charged throughout the film) and both indulge in separate fantasy sequences involving each other. Also, as with all horrors, the main female protagonist always manages to lose her clothing and here Jenny almost adheres to this when the destructive spirit destroys her office whilst in pursuit of her.

Jenny gets to do lots of running about and confesses her guilt to the dull house detective (Moriarty) as the climax of the film approaches. It is only around this point that the viewer can actually enjoy Dark Tower before a wholly damp squib of an ending closes the picture. This is facilitated by Carolyn vanishing after being hounded by the malevolent spirit of her dead husband and we never get to know what happened to her but can only assume involves being in some kind of spiritual limbo.

Utter nonsense but Theodore Bikel as parapsychologist Max and his kooky psychic associate Serge (Kevin McCarthy) provide much unintentional humour and not to spoil the outcome, as if it matters, both meet grizzly deaths along with many others in the film. Another example being the fetishization of Carolyn's obsession with the machinations of the building. At one point blood drips from a window, Jenny sees her late husband in the lift (a facility you most definitely would not want to use because everyone who does, ends up becoming very peculiar thereafter!).

Filmed in Barcelona, Dark Tower is a peculiar little oddity co-written by past-Emmy winner Robert J. Avreck, Ken Blackwell/ Barnett and Ken Wiederhorn. Now here is where things get complicated; Barnett is a pseudonym of original director Freddie Francis who later disowned the film. He, of course, was a distinguished camera operator/ cinematographer/ director and winner of 2 Academy Awards as well as a nominee on many, many occasions. Freddie distanced himself from the released film after early technical effects proved unsatisfactory and his producer promised to show him a rough cut prior to a new SFX team being brought in and the key moments being filmed anew. Regrettably, this never occurred and Francis demanded that his name be removed from the credits of the distributed film. Watch the picture and you will understand his decision. Wiederhorn received a credit as he was brought in to replace him. Francis died in 2007 and received a posthumous tribute at the 2008 Academy Awards show. Dark Tower is not to be confused with the Stephen King book/ film.

Amazon Women on the Moon (1987) 81 mins
'Starring lots of actors.'
Opening cast credits.
Jenny appears very briefly in the Peter Pan Theatre

production skit titled Anthony & Cleopatra and looks fabulous in her Cleo garb. She speaks briefly before literally flying off, stage left. Written by Michael Barrie and Jim Mullholland the sequence was directed by Carl Gottlieb, co-writer of the excellent Steve Martin film The Jerk. He was one of 5 directors on Amazon, with John Landis, another in amongst a group whose work included Police Squad and The Blues Brothers.

A considerable amount of tinkering took place before Amazon Women on the Moon got a cinematic release, subsequent television airing and later video and DVD presentations. Meaning that depending upon which version you see, for example, the 2004 Universal DVD only features the Jenny offering on its deleted scenes 'extras' section of the disc's menu.

Overall, Amazon Women is a fun watch but so fragmented because indubitably some of the 20+ sketches are funnier than others, whilst many outstay their welcome. Werewolf cast member Griffin Dunne stars in a weaker moment amongst a diverse cast which included Michelle Pfeiffer, cult director Russ Meyer, Rosanna Arquette and veteran Ralph Bellamy. Viewers' reaction has been

decidedly mixed and it still divides consensus today; with some loving it and others wondering what they had just watched on screen.

Critical comments:

'Boy, do I love this movie! I'm not saying it didn't have any flaws. I would say about 80% of it was very funny.'
(Ref: Mastamind72, Imdb.co.uk)

'It's pretty easy to get into the sketches. It just feels good for some reason to channel flip through a bunch of random and stupid stuff. Some say it's not funny, because the stuff on there is actually the kind of lame junk you would find on TV, but the humour is there, and it's funny.'
(Ref: Tommy Nelson, Imdb.co.uk)

'…a schizophrenic cocktail of short skits.'
(Ref: pussicato, Imdb.co.uk)

'The film remains fun for fans of B movies but not nearly as funny as I think it tried to be.'
(Rcf: funkyfry, Imdb.co.uk)

'Had a certain celeb- spotting value, but the overriding question in each case was how the hell did they get him/her to appear in this pants? Did they read the script first ?'
(Ref: Superba, lovefilm.co.uk)

'…Irreverent, vulgar and silly and has some hilarious moments and some real groaners.'
(Ref: Variety Movie Guide)

King of the Wind (1989) 102 mins

'One day they will win. First they have to survive.'

A 'U' certificate with a 4m pounds budget from debuting film makers HTV International and set in the 18th century detailing adventures taking place through Tunisia, France and England.

Based upon the book by American-born author Marguerite Henry, King of the Wind was published in 1948 and was just one of many titles by the writer most-famous for Misty of Chincoteague. A prolific writer from a very young age, Ms.Henry wrote animal-based stories and her work continues to be popular. She died in 1997.

Released on the Vestron Video label, its cover description reads: 'From the royal stables of Morocco, to the darkest streets of Paris, to the barren moors of England, no one could break his will to run. The true story of the bond between a mute stable boy and an often-mistreated stallion. It tells of their fight to survive, in a bid to succeed, against all the odds.'

A superb cast was headlined by The Snow Goose star Richard Harris as King George II and Glenda Jackson as Queen Caroline. As well as that, Frank Finlay is Edward Coke and Jenny was cast as Hannah Coke. Enhancing the Jenny connection are Nigel Hawthorne and Anthony Quayle (seen in East of Sudan, many years earlier). An incidental association saw Ralph Bates in a support role (he was in the lead role of the original Dear John series; the American version of which would offer Jenny a frivolous role).

An enjoyable cast with a sappy script. King of the

Wind saw filming in Turkey with its desert location being close to holiday resort Kalkan.

Critical comments:

'The film has more stereotypes than you could shake a stick at, and a script so stiff it ached for a comic cameo…'

(Ref: Brynley Hamer-Jones, Western Mail, 19 May 1990)

'When I saw the movie, I didn't think it captured the spirit of the novel but taken on its own, it's a good horse tale.'

(REF: Staci L.Wilson, Amazon.co.uk)

'Although the screenplay is functional rather than imaginative, it is good natured and full of incident.'

(Ref: Christopher Tookey, Sun.Telegraph, 1990)

Darkman (1990) 91 mins

'I'm in charge here, damn it; let me through!' Jenny remonstrating in amongst the chaos following the disappearance of her patient in the film of Darkman.

A comic book feel pervades this dark action-thriller from Evil Dead creator Sam Rami (he also co-developed early drafts of the screenplay). Liam Neeson fills the title role as a doctor who becomes his own superhero and in whom the audience is fully behind after seeing what happens to him. An 18 certificate, Darkman has a good cast which numbered Australian actor Colin Friels and Coen Brothers regular Frances McDormand.

Its musical score was composed by Batman muso Danny Elfman and completes the comic book feel. There are lots of stunning visual moments and Jenny makes an un-credited cameo as the chief medic within a specialist burns department treating the brutalized Westlake (Neeson). She enters at about twenty minutes into the story and basically offers a brief summary of his condition before looking on bemusedly at his sudden departure through a window (he's off to reek his vengeance).

Rami gives a knowing nod to horror fans with a wordless cameo from American Werewolf of London director John Landis. He is seen as a bespectacled associate within Jenny's medical group visiting Neeson. Rami was a big comic book fan as a youngster and Darkman really demonstrates this fact well. An illustrative series of stories has since been published and sequels to the film have followed.

Critical comments:

'Despite occasional silliness…has more wit, pathos and visual flamboyance than is usual in contemporary shockers.'

(Ref: Variety Movie Guide 1999)

'A frenetic funhouse ride that has you laughing and screaming at the same time.'
(Ref: Joe Brown, WashingtonPost.com).

Child's Play 2 (1990) 84 mins

'It's only a doll.'

This Don Mancini written sequel to the 1988 original retained its director John Lafia (who co-wrote this) and continues to tick all the pre-requisite boxes common to the horror genre. Namely: 1) a big, creepy house; 2) a thumping soundtrack and 3) a killer that seems invincible. Childs Play 2 has all of these but has its tongue firmly in its cheek even if the climactic scene is stomach- churning. The plot never really matters in these kinds of films, suffice to say that the spirit of a serial killer is still trapped within the cutesy Tommy, a freckled doll in the 'Good Guy' product range. Chucky is back and comes hunting once

morc for Andy (Alex Vincent), the little lad being the latest youngster to be fostered by affluent Chicago couple Joanne (Jenny) and Phil (Gerrit Graham). Jenny puts on an American twang to her accent but we just know that disaster is going to call: and soon it does. The idea is well carried out and the film is pointedly black in its humour. Its anticipating, menacing soundtrack precipitates the horror and within the first hour both the couple are murdered. For Jenny watchers, her character bites the dust via a particularly gruesome fashion at 52 minutes in. On a quizzical note, we realise that suspension of disbelief is paramount in this genre, but why do horror flicks always feature a thunderstorm? (But then Shakespeare used such dramatic techniques as do all contemporary film makers) The one in Child's Play 2 is so overtly animated that the scene makes the characters appear as if in a state of a perpetual passport photo booth suspended animation. Flash after flash, one evening sees Jenny comforting the new arrival at her enormous wooden home accompanied by a tempest outside; yet the bedroom curtains remain wide open! Child's Play 2 suffered uncomfortable associations with the Bulger murder at the time of its release and Jenny has been quoted as regarding the finished film as boring. But I would have to disagree, it's just silly.

Critical comments:

'This second film is just good enough to be the one that cemented his status among the horror franchises that wouldn't die.'
(Ref: stomptokyo.com)

'…an inevitable sequel that's not as good as its progenitor, but better than most movies with the numbers 2 through 8 in their titles.'
(Ref: Richard Harrington, Washington Post)

'Definately the best in the series, more chucky, more gore, more fun.'
(Ref: J.Goind, CD Universe)
'Offers nothing of any real distinction to be a satisfactory sequel. (Ref: Tweeder16, Amazon.com)
'…is another case of rehashing the few novel elements of an original to the point of utter numbness.'
(Ref: Variety Movie Guide 1999).

Freddie as F.R.0.7 (1992) 86 mins
'You rotten stinker!'
Jenny as 'Daffers' during a moment of peril.
'The world's most lovable new animated superhero!'
Billed by its British makers as 'An amazing fantasy of a new kind', Freddie was set to be the first in a series of animated features starring Ben Kingsley as the elite French intelligence agent. Alas, the sequels never happened and we only get to enjoy Kingsley and the Kung Fu-chopping delight that is Daphne aka 'Daphers'. Jenny's gadget-developer character actually does resemble the actress as do Freddie and the Brian Blessed evildoer. Only in her red-headed animated form, Jenny is somewhat more curvaceous (what is it about animated films that Freddie as F.R.0.7 or Freddie the Frog as it is known in America persist in having females constructed in this manner?) Her character along with the others was created by a team of 250 animators working to bring the story to life for the London-based Hollywood Road Film Productions based in Battersea. As is the norm with these types of productions, the voice tracks were recorded first and the characters drawn up later.

The plot in animated features is perfunctory but storywriters Jon Aceveski and actor David Ashton do make the story personal to Freddie and we get a final confrontation in keeping with its Bond comparison. The film does have a bit of playful jingoism with stereotypical blundering 'men from the ministry' and wooden tops and some snide teasing of Freddie being French but all in all it proves a good wheeze. The cast are terrific in between a number of songs composed and sung by the disparate likes of Boy George, Holly Johnson and Grace Jones.

Also providing his vocal talents is Nigel Hawthorne. And of course, Jenny and Ben Kingsley were again working together after both featuring in the excellent television adaptation of Silas Marner in 1985.

Writing in his book The Animated Movie Guide Jerry Beck states that the makers of Freddie went out of business after the commercial failure of the film. Some minutes of a sequel were not to see the light of day and plans for a third feature were shelved.

Critical comments:

'…an illustration on how *not* to make an animated film…an awful script, boring visuals, pedestrian animation, dull colours, stupid ideas, terrible songs, music, and background…'
(Ref: Jerry Beck, The Animated Movie Guide).

'…a hotchpotch of half-baked ideas ransacked from Disney, Bond and, at a guess, cult shows like The Avengers and Dr Who. The most intriguing notion is that by stealing historic monuments, the Snake Queen hopes to extract the country's life force and plunge the population into inertia. The rest is lame jokes and outmoded stereotypes.'
(Ref: TCH, Time Out Film Guide)

'…of such mindless banality you wonder how they all got involved [the cast]. Freddie the Frog should have been drowned…at the very outset of this mind-numbing fable.'
(Ref: Sheridan Morley, Sunday Express, 16 August 1992)

'Freddie remains mediocre in the extreme'.
(Ref: Marshall Julius, What's on London, 1992).

Blue Juice (1995) 94 mins

'She's a goddess!'
Worzel's lad Sean Pertwee shines in this smashingly enjoyable piece of fluff performed by a handsome cast with much aplomb. Also included is a sultry Catherine Zeta Jones and cockneyed-up Ewan McGregor (with an accent straight arrrtahh drama school). You just know that most of the cast could not have been further removed from the characters that they play in Blue Juice but it doesn't spoil the enjoyment of this vibrantly shot feature. Set in picturesque Cornwall, it tries to be the Brit equivalent of The Big Surf (1978) but is laughable up against such comparisons. Still, lots of beautiful shots promote the ocean and landscape so succinctly that it makes you want to get on the next train down there. Jenny comes into the story about a group of former mates from London struggling with responsibility and maturity (they are all of thirty!) against the irresponsibility of youth. Miss Agutter comes on screen at about 47 minutes in during a dialogue-free scene where she appears at a tearoom where Terry (Peter Gunn) and (Ewan McGregor) visit to sample a traditional Cornish tea (cream cakes and all). The only difference being that the former is unwittingly high on drugs and hugely aroused at seeing a smiling Jenny here cast as an actress from a telly show that the lads used to watch as children. You can entirely empathize with their excitement at seeing her before their very eyes as a now adult Guinevere (Jenny) looks very self-assured in a pretty dress resplendent in pearls. Just what is it about a

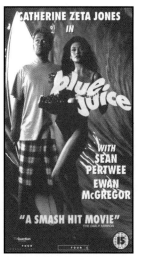

woman of a certain age wearing these that speaks so much? I think it represents class, maturity and confidence in a clear statement.

As Terry, actor Peter Gunn provides much of the comedic moments in Blue Juice and the film appears dated already when the lads attend a beachfront rave organized by Chloe (Jones) who wants to settle down against the wishes of a worried JC (Pertwee) who doesn't want to see her change with the responsibility in keeping up with pub-running Terry.

Jenny resurfaces a little later via TV screen where she features in a re-run of her old telly role that the lads used to watch only now Terry is dressed as the Silver Surfer character (you have to see the film to understand why). Still high as a kite, he believes that she is literally calling for his help and sets out to rescue her.

It is a very brief but witty scene and whilst the main characters struggle with various clichéd but salient issues, Jenny comes back into the film towards the end. Looking elegant and very beautiful as the adult Mary Fenton, the foolhardy Terry appears outside her house astride a horse, with another for her. She immediately pooh-poohs his idea but with a twinkle in her disbelieving eye.

I might be being pedantic here but a question that I ask is how does the lovelorn Tel know where to find Guinevere (Jenny) once he returns in readiness to ride off into the sunset? After first seeing her lovely smiling vision at the tea room, whilst unknowingly tripping out on an Ecstasy tab supplied by his mate McGregor (he later discovers that it was not the paracetomol that he had believed!) I guess that Jenny most probably owned the posh tearooms in which we see her?

She looks sumptuous with a glint in her eye and "I'm-not-the-person-off-telly" reasoning to a besotted Terry whilst trying to enjoy her latter-day anonymity. Following its initial cinematic release, Blue Juice was re-packaged for DVD with Zeta-Jones and Ewan McGregor promoted as its stars (the latter is only really a co-star here). In a correspondence with the author, Peter Gunn remembers the hedonistic period of filming Blue Juice on location in St.Ives somewhat hazily but has a clear recollection of meeting Jenny. 'When Jenny arrived (on set) we were on our best behaviour. For me though it was one of those moments when you meet someone you have seen loads in loads of film and the reality of that person is even better; she was so nice to us and very easy to talk with and have a laugh with. You must remember that we were all young, male; (the cast) had all bonded through partying and work so it was doubly hard for Jenny to fit in. But she was lovely.' Peter also recalls another incident similar to that recounted by Red Dwarf actor Robert Llewellyn, appertaining to the physical appeal of Ms.Agutter. 'One amusing occasion we were filming in a remote cove and the unit base was on top of the cliff looking out to sea: it was gorgeous. As always, filming there was a lot of hanging about but we were good at filling the time; kite flying, chilling out, chatting with our "surfer doods"…Anyway, we sat on the grass having a laugh and out of the make-up van comes Jenny dressed as Guinevere in her long white shift and stood talking to us. Again, it was one of those moments for as she stood there in front of us we all realized that the sun was behind her and had made her shift see-through! It was a bit of a Princess Di moment. For me, seeing Jenny like that was a bit of a thrill because I had seen Walkabout not long since!' A bashful Mr. Gunn concluded, 'I don't think that she knew the effect she had on us or that her dress has become see-through…but she was just really nice. By the way, your review was spot on: Someone told me it was a cult film in Germany and Australia. I still get spotted as Terry (his screen stealing character) all these years later.'

Critical comments:

'In the wake of Four Weddings & a Funeral and Shallow Grave, comes another sparkling entertainment.'
(Ref: Empire film magazine)

'This British youth comedy, first released in 1995, has arrived on these shores past its expiry date thanks to its minor star appeal: Ewan McGregor (Trainspotting, Shallow Grave), the pretty Catherine Zeta Jones (soon to be seen in Zorro) and Sean Pertwee (Event Horizon). The movie seems much, much longer than its 90-minute running time…a movie recommended primarily for nostalgic Cornish people who might enjoy the landscape. Or, anyone curious enough to see what the British version of Beach Blanket Bingo might look like.'
(Ref: www.theglobeandmail.com)

The Parole Officer (2001) 94 mins

'No, I'm Victor's wife.'

At a little over half-hour into what was Steve Coogan's film debut in a starring role, Jenny makes the first of her fleeting appearances in this enjoyable British heist comedy with a difference. The basic premise being nerdy probation officer Simon (Alan Partridge man Coogan) witnessing a murder by a corrupt copper. As the probation officer of the title, oddly revised for American audiences, he enlists the help of a disparate band of former criminals to help retrieve a security tape that captured the dastardly deed. The only problem being that it is securely procured in a bank safety deposit box. So he seeks out Vincent (a glowing cameo by Omar Sherif, no less) to complete the gang to snatch the

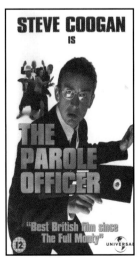

incriminating evidence, only to be shocked with the discovery that he has died.

This news is conveyed by Victor's wife, played by Jenny, looking lovely in her garb of grey, closely-cropped hair.

Her other scenes involve no dialogue but offer a surprise as she and Mr Sharif appear on screen riding a tandem as the film reaches its close. Of course, all things turn out fine for Coogan and co. (he co-wrote the script with sometime writing partner Henry Normal) and right at the close, Jenny is spotted in disguise as a W.P.C alongside Inspector Omar, as they drive off with a bag full of the corrupt detective's dosh.

Good fun and with moments of laugh-out-loud humour mainly provided by your man Coogan.

Critical comments:

'A feel-good comedy caper movie…done pretty slickly, and the protagonist is invariably hilarious.' (Ref: Amazon.co.uk)

At Dawning (2001) 12 mins

Released by Real Time Short Films under their 'Small Wonders - Volume 1: A showcase of the best British short films' banner, At Dawning was one amongst a dozen eclectic shorts contained on a single DVD release. Celia Imrie, Jenny's screen sister in a 2005 episode of Agatha Christie's Poirot, appears in another of the films on the disc. Jenny was cast in the part of a woman desperately trying to leave the flat of a one-night-stand without being discovered. Unfortunately for her, the sight of a man stuck in a tree outside the window does not help her ease of exit. It transpires that the distressed man, portrayed by award-winning actor Yvan Attal, is heartbroken and suicidal after discovering the infidelity of his partner who lives in the flat above.

Former ad man Martin Jones directed and worked with actress Emma Bernard on this picking up a trio of awards: the Golden Berlin Bear for Best Short film at the Berlin International Film Festival (2002), the Prix UIP Valladolid (European Short Film) award at the Valladolid International Film Festival (2002) & Best Cinematography at the Capalbio Cinema Awards (2002).

Since completing this dark comedy, Martin is developing a number of projects including a full-length feature film appertaining to At Dawning provisionally titled It Never Happened. Therefore, perhaps Jenny may reprise her role at some point. The people at RealTime Short Films distribute profits made from DVD sales back to the film makers and attempt to offer future creatives an opportunity to bring their work to fruition. To find out more, visit their website - www.realtimeshortfilms.co.uk

Critical comments:

'…the dialog is great and everything works well. There are plenty of things I didn't mention, as I don't want to spoil the film. Regardless, the acting, writing and direction are simply lovely and it's nice

to see an older Jenny Agutter in film: I haven't seen her in at least a decade or more and she looks simply smashing.'
(Ref: planktonrules, Isbn.com)

Heroes and Villains (2006) 101 mins

'What does love mean to you?'
So asks Jack (David Raymond) in this un-taxing British feature film from first-time director Selwyn Roberts. Raymond, who also wrote the screenplay, leads a group of mates which includes James Cordon, in a morally-dubious, 'honey pot' capital-making venture. The company offers male and female stooges to test the fidelity of a partner whose behaviour has caused doubts in the mind of their significant other.
Jenny is first seen on screen almost an hour into the story, cast as Jack's mother June, with Roy Marsden, as her husband and his father. Initially she is seen in almost silhouette form when Jack brings his new, posh girlfriend home for his father's birthday. Alas, we only see her in 3 or 4 scenes. The most prescient being the footage wherein her own fidelity is unknowingly gaged by her son's company, unbeknownst to him. It is a fine scene and proves a memorable moment in a passably lightweight, south London-set feature. Leading man Raymond got the germ of an idea that transpired to be the film storyline through his own real-life circumstances. He worked hard to raise the £1.1million budget through his own connections in the Investment banking trade (the money being found through personal equity).
Critical comments:
'Good gags and terrific performances.'
(Ref: Matthew Turner, viewlondon.co.uk)
'…quickly abandons its initial early promise and descends into a laboured sob story lifted from an episode of Hollyoaks. Pretty uninspiring stuff.'
(Ref: Mike Barnard, futuremovies.co.uk)
'I certainly recommend this film, particularly for couples. It was tragically underrated when it came out.' (Ref: J2theFizzle, Play.com)
'It has a decent enough cast on paper, The production values look fine. But nothing in it comes together - or rather, what does come together is pretty alarming, and, in the end, just baffling.' (Ref: Peter Bradshaw, guardian.co.uk)
'…roughly patched together by producer-turned-director Selwyn Roberts, and the faults are underlined by explanatory voiceover. All this, added to dreary dialogue, total lack of chemistry between insipid romantic leads, is enough to make you lose your faith in love and British filmmaking.'
(Ref: Stella Papamichael, bbc.co.uk)

Irina Palm (2007) 103 mins

'Oh for god's sake Mags, it's you we're talking about. It's not as if it's anything remotely interesting.'

An acerbic-sounding Jenny in the film.

With a real pan-European mix of acting/ production talent, Irina Palm was co-written by Martin Herron and Phillipe Blastand and directed by Sam Garbarski.

Jenny appears on screen within the first five minutes as a malevolent friend of the dowdy Mags (an excellent Marianne Faithfull) receiving an 'and Jenny Agutter' credit on the opening titles.

It is a brave performance from Ms.Faithfull as a mature woman whose grandson is desperately in need of specialized medical treatment. The only problem being for the pot less family is that he needs to be taken to Australia quickly where such treatment can be given. Circumstance decreeing action, a naïve Mags somehow ends up working in London's Soho sex trade albeit in a most peculiar fashion. Wherein she discovers she has a much sought after talent that proves mightily popular with the punters. Despite her bemused displeasure, Mags continues working due to the fact that she can earn a lot of money very quickly to pass on to aid her grandchild.

Initially concerned for her friend, Jane (Jenny) and her like-minded friends are shocked to discover the truth about her 'secret life' and the scene where the denouement is revealed is a joy. In a village where everyone seems to know everybody else's business, Mags takes great delight in telling her so-called friends and its hilarious to hear Jenny say 'wank'. She proves to be a most unpleasant piece of work and not a true friend as all is revealed later when her affair with Mags' late husband is disclosed. Described as 'tragic, comic' by Garbarski, Irina Palm (the pseudonym given to Mags in the sex trade) makes for quite difficult viewing. However, the main character is quite something and her social withdrawal and difficulties are reminiscent of such thought-provoking films as Love Liza, Broken Flowers, Dirty Pretty Things & About Schmidt.

Critical comments:

'It's a truly ludicrous film, almost a laugh a line, that sets out to be the Mrs. Warren's Profession of our time, but turns out to be Cranford meets Confessions of a Manual Worker.'
(Ref: Philip French, The Observer, 15/06/2008)

'A gob smackingly awful British film - awful in the way that somehow only British films can be: our TV drama, of whatever quality, is never as creaky, naive, badly written and flatulent as this.'
(Ref: Peter Bradshaw, The Guardian, 13/06/2008)

'There's a heart-warming quality that softens the hardcore setting.'
(Ref: Kat Brown - www.empireonline.com)

'A brave idea and a brave movie.'
Cast member Miki Manojlovic.

The Magic Door (2007) 90 mins

'You think I would let a stupid troll spoil my plans?!'

Jenny in The Magic Door.

Ms Agutter received top billing in this children's fantasy drama which takes some time to get going. She put's in a fun performance that seems more suited to pantomime than a film. In fact, The Magic Door, written and directed by Paul Matthews suffers from not knowing where to pitch itself. It is also handicapped by some laden acting from a wooden Patsy Kensit alongside Jenny's Invisibles telly co-star, Antony Head. Jenny commented in a BBC interview whilst filming The Invisibles, 'I did a film with Anthony which I don't think it saw the light of day. It didn't make it to the big screen which is sad.'

The Head/ Kensit duo play the parents of two youngsters embroiled in a battle between the black witch (Ms Agutter) and seemingly everybody else. First sight of Jenny proves quite shocking and it's difficult not to laugh when you see her clad in a bad, Cher-like wig (with purple highlights, no less). However, she seems to be enjoying herself and so if you go with it, she provides much of the humour in the film. Sadly, the cast seems to be acting against each other, some panto-like, others as if they are in a bad soap opera or goodness knows what: such is the discrepancy of performance quality. As the black witch, it is a role that presents itself as a nasty piece of work for Jenny, with some fun moments against a dialogue such as, 'I'd sooner have you fairies in charge than the witch.'

Critical comments:

'Big names and great effects do not a great movie make!' (REF: lifeschool389107, Imdb.co.uk)

Intercom (2008) 10 mins

'Looking out for you.'

A captivating-looking Jenny stars in this drama co-written by producer/director Mark Gutteridge and Aidan Lean. As the home-loving Mrs. Henley, her character prefers to read a book or watch the telly than anything more strenuous until the appearance of a new tenant in her complex causes concerns.

Simon (Marc Warren) does not fit in with the likes of those at the building such as Mr Smith (David Calder, who acted with Jenny in a 2002 episode of Spooks) and Mr Collins (David Garry) who all like things just they way they are. So the new arrival is constantly monitored by those within in this absorbing short feature.

Jenny made herself available for a days' filming and features heavily in the wordless trailer which works marvellously well in giving a view into what the film is all about. At the time of writing, Intercom was being edited in readiness for its commerical release.

Glorious 39 (2009) 124 mins

'It's not always a good place to go, the past.'
Film poster strapline.

Receiving a November 2009 theatrical release, Jenny provided a supporting role on this rare feature film outing for celebrated theatre/ television creative Stephen Poliakoff (who also directs).

Set in both the present day and during war time, this thriller was shot across 6 weeks on locations in Norfolk, London and elsewhere in readiness for release in 2009: the 70th anniversary of the outbreak of World War II.

Premiered at the Toronto Film Festival in 2009, praise for the film was trumpeted by Piers Handling, who described it as 'a wonderfully unsettling film...supported by a superb cast of some of the finest English actors.' [Torontotiff.net] Indeed, Jenny was in the cast alongside the likes of Bill Nighy, Julie Christie and Christopher Lee who seemingly queued up to appear in a feature with a running time of a little over 2 hours. Jenny features as Maud Keyes, the wife of MP Bill Nighy. Made with a not incredibly-expensive $6m budget, Glorious 39 was originally titled '1939'. Its screenplay is also available in paperback. Jenny had previously acted in Poliakoff's theatrical piece Breaking the Silence back in 1985 (see the theatre section for full details).

jenny on the telly

Alexander Graham Bell (1965) un/kwn mins

This BBC TV production marked the first small-screen appearance by Jenny in a biographical work about the life of the great Scottish scientist/ inventor/ innovator. She features as the youngest sister in a show directed by The Railway Children helmer Julia Smith. Jenny's film co-star and pal Judy Geeson also appears, as does the lovely Francesca Annis. Oddly, all three are omitted from official cast credits for a show that was shown in February 1965. Bell was played by Alec McCowen, an actor with a strong theatrical pedigree.

The Newcomers (1965) 25 mins

There are a small number of creative people that Jenny has repeatedly worked with across her career, with Michael York and Peter Finch immediately springing to mind. Here, in this twice-weekly soap devised to compete with Coronation Street, the Jenny associations are myriad. The aforementioned Julia Smith also directed episodes of The Newcomers across its life span of 1965-69. Scripted by actor/writer/producer Colin Morris, Jenny acted in a single episode as Kirsty Kerr.

The main premise of the show, which ran across some 430 episodes, detailed the lives of the Cooper family as they adapt to a new life away from their London roots. Judy Geeson and Jeremy Bulloch were cast as siblings Maria and Phillip Cooper, respectively. Ms.Geeson and Jenny were friends off-screen and worked on a number of films together. Whilst Jeremy, who like Jenny Agutter, found fame as a child actor, would later act in Number One, Longing. Number Two, Regret. The Newcomers was shown primarily on Tuesday and Thursday but alas only a mere handful of episodes remain today. Jenny's appearance went out in October 1965.

Ballerina (1966) un/kwn mins

'When I was little, both my parents made me feel special but I was, thankfully, never made to feel that what I was doing was hugely important. I got the role in the Walt Disney film [Ballerina] and I thought I was the bee's knees. When you get back to school, they remind you terribly quickly that you're not.'

Jenny from an interview.

Miss. Agutter acted in this two-part, 1966 television show from the Disney stable whilst eleven after being trained at the Elmhurst Ballet School, Surrey, aged 9. Both episodes were directed by the American-born Norman Campbell with the basic story premise seeing a young ballet student in Denmark succeeding in spite of her mother's protestations. Co-written by prolific screenwriter Casey Robinson and Robert Westerby, with an original idea by Peter Schnitzler and partly shot at the Royal Theater, Copenhagen. Its director made his name as a successful adaptor of ballet stories for the small-screen and remembers Walt Disney liking the finished work very much. Ballerina subsequently came under many titles such as Disney's Wonderful World aka The Disney Sunday Movie aka The Magical World of Disney. aka The Wonderful World of Disney aka Walt Disney aka Walt Disney Presents aka Walt Disney's Wonderful World of Color. Now, its last title is interesting in that all the episodes made for the U.S channel ABC were filmed in colour, even though they aired in black and white (and later shown in colour via another channel). I am uncertain as to whether Ballerina was one of the projects released theatrically outside of the States but for its American presentation it was aired as a two-parter. Jenny's character was called Ingrid Jensen and the show aired in March 1966 as part of the 12th series. Walt Disney died in April 1967 and some years later, Jenny returned to the Disney fold for the feature film presentation Amy.

A photograph of Jenny alongside Mr Disney and other youngsters exists.

Long After Summer (1967) un/kwn mins

Also known as Boy Meets Girl: Long after

Summer, this telly episode (number 10 in the first series) was screened on BBC1 in October 1967. Jenny was cast as Johanna whose father was British actor John Collin and the two coincidentally repeated the same casting in the 1968 feature film Star! Its American scripter, Dale Wasserman, had previously written musicals and other television productions.

The Railway Children (1968)

'It is quite old-fashioned. It's wonderful but it is a different time.'

Jenny talking about the series on the BBC TV Breakfast show.

The Railway Children was originally published in serial form in the London Magazine (1905) prior to its appearance as a novel in 1906. Born in London back in 1858, its author Edith Nesbit, known as 'E. Nesbit' on the book cover, would surely be very proud to know that her seminal work still appeals to generations more than a century since its publication. As for Jenny's association, she would act in the 1968 BBC dramatisation, more of which you can read below, by which time the story had already seen 2 previous interpretations on the station in 1951 and 1957 respectively. That much-missed delight Jackanory also dramatised it in 1981 and Jenny has narrated the book in an audio format too (as did her film mother Dinah Sheridan).

Our interest commences with the 7 episodes timed at 25 minutes each which aired on the BBC from May to June 1968. Aged sixteen at the time, Jenny plays Robert aka Bobbie by those around her and followed Anneke Wills and Marion Chapman in previous productions.

1 The Visitors : The opening credits to each episode of this charming black and white adaptation from Denis Constanduros, a scriptwriter with a mass of television experience up until his death in 1978, sees the camera pan from a steam train up a bank to where three children sit on a fence. The children in order of age, are Roberta, played by Jenny, Neil McDermott as Peter and Gillian Bailey as the precocious Phyllis. Miss Bailey proves especially endearing and the young actress went on to appear in a lot of telly roles, with the Double Deckers her most recognisable. By 1991 she had quit acting and was, in recent times, a lecturer at Royal Holloway College, Surrey. Master McDermott appears to have not continued acting after this project.

The Railway Children was an atypical Sunday tea-time fair and was directed by Eastenders co-creator, Julia Smith. Apparently shot live, The Visitors introduced the Faraday family to viewers back in a Victorian world where this particular brood are, on the outside, well-off; with a maid addressing father (a suitably stuffy Frederick Treves) as 'master' and in the Dinah Sheridan role of mother, Ann Castle brings much warmth to a sympathetic role.

Jenny's performance as Bobbie, or 'miss goody-goody' as her young brother teases, starts of somewhat nervously and as has been stated that the series was recorded live so no wonder she appears anxious. All shoulder-length hair in tails, complimented by a centre parting and bows she looks very sweet; not quite an adult but neither a child still either. Plot wise, mother has to manage without her husband and the family is forced to economise by accepting a kind offer of use of a cottage in the country from q literary friend. Their arrival there proves a culture shock and is very reminiscent of similar scenes in The Amazing Mr Blunden (1972), directed by Lionel Jeffries.

2 The Coalminers : The warmth in the children's relationships is demonstrated as they begin to explore their new, rural environment. Their fascination with the railway blossoms and with the 'fiery, green dragon' as Jenny perceptibly terms one of the steam locos.

The children meet Perks, the station attendant, defined by Nesbit as 'a friendly sort with no nonsense about him.' Here he is smashingly portrayed by Gordon Gostelow. Joining together, the young Faradays decide to relocate some coal from the station bunker so that mother can be warm when she writes stories to sell to make some much-needed money. Unfortunately, Perks catches them and they face the wrath of 'his nibbs' the stationmaster (atypically portrayed by Brian Hayes). Their financial plight is revealed and they are ultimately forgiven.

3 The Message :Roberta, Peter and Phyllis continue their daily ritual of waving to passengers on the passing trains and in particular, an old gentleman that always returns their greetings. Mother falls ill and the youngsters hatch a plan to provide her with items recommended by the village doctor but asking their 'old gentleman' to help. Here the excellent plotting of the script and E. Nesbit's original work shines brightly. Everything is tied together and becomes clear as the story progresses.

The train passenger, a Mr Inglewood, acquiesces and a hamper duly arrives at the family cottage 'Three Chimneys' (although the series clearly did not have an architecturally correct property to use and as such the house exterior is never fully revealed). When their proud mother recovers she is furious to learn that they have asked a stranger to help and lecturers them.

4 The Foreign Gentleman : The arrival of a penniless and sickly stranger to the village station causes much consternation amongst the locals (or should I say xenophobia). Mrs Faraday manages to converse in French with him and it is revealed that he is a famous Russian author in search of his exiled wife. And as comedian Ben Elton used to say, a 'little bit of politics' is introduced to the plot. Once again the children communicate their concerns to Inglewood who being a capable man, sorts everything out. In a moving final scene, after Perks has brought up some post and old newspapers for the children to read, Bobbie

discovers the truth about their father's absence but keeps the discover from her young sister and mother. It transpires that he is Civil Servant that has breached the Official Secrets Act and had been sent to prison as a consequence.

5 The Secret : Bobbie's agonising over the disclosure of the wretched truth of her father's 'trip abroad' is unfastened upon her mother insisting that she tell her what is wrong. This episode also includes the famous landslide scene albeit in a pared-down form. It nonetheless retains the drama of the latter, more expansive film version. Suffice to say that red petticoats still feature prominently (not that we can tell from the black and white photography) as the children attempt to warn the oncoming train of the danger of a displaced tree which is covering the line. In the film, there is that fabulous 'Keep off the tracks, Bobbie!' moment as Jenny's character literally stands in the way to prevent an accident. Here it is slightly different and an end with her fainting at the side of the tracks after the crash has been avoided. Again, it presents a very exciting moment as is repeated in the film.

6 The Rescue : The Faraday children are rewarded with a public acknowledgement of thanks from the railway company at the local station. And in another exciting climax, Bobbie and a young lad find themselves in a darkened tunnel with an impending train scheduled to soon be approaching.

Here we see Jenny's Roberta clearly demonstrating an attraction towards the boy. Just as the Saturday morning Flash Gordon serials would end on a cliff-hanger, so does this episode.

7 The Meeting : 'Daddy, my daddy!'

The petticoat theme; such a Victorian symbol of confined femininity, is creatively utilised by Bobbie to aid the discomfort of the boy's damaged ankle whilst the two battle to get out of the tunnel. Plot construction of course decrees that they escape safely and the identity of the injured laddie is revealed as being the nephew of the trusted Mr Inglewood (Joseph O'Conor).

Having sought his counsel in regards to the plight of their father, it is Bobbie that has a wonderful surprise within an episode which Jenny comes into her own. Unbeknownst to the stoic youngster, her 'perfect' father has been pardoned and arrives on the train coming into the station. That famous quote is voiced by Jenny and we the audience give a cheer! Lovely stuff, simply shot and very effective.

The Great Inimitable Mr. Dickens (1970) un/knwn mins

Written to commemorate the-then centenary since his the death of thegreat writer, producer/ director Ned Sherrin co-scripted this television film with Caryl Brahms. Best recalled for the seminal 1960s show That Was the Week That Was, Sherrin was able to draw upon a marvellous cast which included Joan Greenwood, Patrick Cargill and Anthony Hopkins as Charles Dickens. Jenny was cast alongside her future screen father in Sweet William (1980) Arthur Lowe, also part of the theatrical cast of The Tempest in 1974. Dame Sybil Thorndike, Ms.Greenwood and Stanley Holloway also starred in virtually their final acting roles. The irrepressible Freddie Jones, another future Jenny co-star, puts in an appearance too. An additional dame, Gladys Cooper, shares a brief scene with Jenny via a screenplay which weaved autobiographical elements from Dickens' novels which were then acted out by the sterling team of actors. Sherrin had his cast run-through the script prior to a full dress rehearsal and then the actual filming of the production. Sadly, such was the ineptitude of the BBC back in the late-1960s/70s that the master tape recording of this production was wiped and is forever lost. Welsh actor and now a naturalized American citizen, Anthony Hopkins, was BAFTA-nominated for his role. Jenny is listed as playing the mulitple roles of Maria, Mary and Ellen Ternan.

The Cherry Orchard - Play of the Month (1971) unknown mins

Written by the great Russian dramatist Anton Chekov, The Cherry Orchard is a four-act comedy set on a country estate. Even though it was intended to be played as a comedy, Stanislavski directed it as a tragedy. It was originally presented at the Moscow Art Theatre in January 1904 and has since seen may adaptations all over the world.
Jenny was cast in the part of Anya, the teen-aged daughter of landowner Madame Liubov Andreievna Ranevskaya. Her mother is a widow desperately trying to save her Russian estate and the cherry orchard therein.
Directed by Cedric Messina, an old hand at producing and directing, Jenny was in amongst a pristine cast which included Celia Johnson and Edward Woodward.
Originally on the BBC in December '71 as the latest presentation in the highly-regarded Play of the Month slot.

The Ten Commandments (1971) un/knwn mins

Little is known about this Alan Prior-scripted episode titled 'As Many as are here present' in which Jenny played Bess Clark, one of four in the Clark family. It was made for Yorkshire TV.

The Wild Duck - Play of the Month (1971) un/knwn mins

Jenny featured prominently in a couple of these BBC 1 dramas which began their run back in 1965 and continued well on into the 1980s. Her first role to be shown was as Hedvig Ekdal in The Wild Duck (premiered in March '71) followed by another performance in The Cherry Orchard in December that same year.

Lots of now well-established actors appeared in more than one of the films in this renowned series which initially went out on a Tuesday evening before changing to a Sunday night slot later on. In essence, the films were predominantly adaptations of well-known classic works with a few original pieces also in the mix.

Its director Alan Bridges also directed Jenny in another BBC play, Shelley, however this Ibsen tragedy was adapted by Max Faber.

Jenny received some positive reviews for her involvement and featured alongside Denholm Elliott, Rosemary Leach, Christopher Benjamin and Derek Godfrey. Very well performed by its cast, The Wild Duck displaces an idyllic life with an impending emotional explosion that affects all around. After a long wait, it has now been made available on DVD. The Wild Duck was the 49th production in the highly-regarded Play of the Month slot and remains one of the least produced Ibsen play.

Shelley (1972) 75 mins

Alan Bridges had recently worked with Jenny on The Wild Duck;an experienced television director, he also directed films, namely The Shooting Party (1985) which featured Sir John Gielgud in a memorable role. The renowned Shakespearian actor would later headline the theatrical cast of The Tempest which gave Jenny a role as Miranda. Dramatist John Elliot set his story about the Romantic poet Shelley in contemporary times and Jenny's future co-star from The Survivor (1980), Robert Powell took the leading role here. Jenny was cast as his wife Mary, the author of the classic gothic novel Frankenstein (1818). Peter Bowles complimented the cast as Byron and the piece was shown on the BBC in July 1972.

A House in Regent Place (1973) 26 mins

'You'll get me into trouble!' Jenny to her beau John (Martin C.Thurley)

Set in a Brighton house across four different time frames, writer Roy Russell presents the vastly opposing lives of the occupants therein. A collection of 4 episodes were made: The Barrier (1914),

Why Weren't We Warned? (1938), Mrs Tycoon (1958) and House Proud (1974).

Released on DVD in 2009, Jenny stars in the opening story as the beautiful, young Elizabeth, 'the daughter of the house,' owned by her parents, the Merriot-Brownes. Coming from a well-off family, the property is used as a convalescent home for injured officers involved in the early brutalities of World War I.

Made by the now-defunct Southern television franchise, the drama featured a lovely piano-based theme by Harry South.

Jenny's twenty-one year-old character, all shoulder-length brown hair, shoe-length skirt tied to her thin waist soon catches the attention of many of the men around her. However, she only has eyes for one of them: Mather (played by Thurley) a man from a working-class background diametrically opposed to her own.

The distinctions look as if they will quash any lasting relationship until Jenny's spirited young woman spouts to her plum-mouthed mother, 'What he says is more important than his accent.' The two romantic leads play well together and the episode concludes with the lovers planning a life in unity. The remaining stories do not feature the same characters but the final episode does include a portrait of Elizabeth (Jenny) in a photograph album compiled by the couple owning the house in the early-1970s. Directed by Derek Martinus, A House in Regent Place was shown as 4 x 25 minutes episodes. Jeremy Clyde, later seen in other Jenny Agutter projects School Play and The Alan Clarke Diaries, also features here.

Thriller (1974) 73 mins
'The spine chilling 70s anthology.'
DVD copy line.
'My strongest memory is of the fact that (he) and I would have terrible bouts of giggles, which at one point stopped filming for at least half an hour I am ashamed to say.'
Jenny speaking about making the episode of Thriller with George Chakiris.
(Ref: BBC Four Cinema)
With story titles including 'Night Time is for killing' and 'Someone at the top of the stairs' I imagine that its original telly audience knew just what it was in for back in the 1970s. A mammoth 43 episodes across 6 series were made of this Brian Clemens deviscd horror series which ran from 1973-76 on ITV. Each story had a twist in its tail and featured some past and future Jenny co-stars; namely Robert Powell, Denholm Elliot, Michael Kitchen, Peter Bowels and Francesca Annis. Jenny's involvement in this popular and critically well-received drama serial saw her act in 'Kiss me and die', episode 3 in the second series. It was broadcast in February 1974 and written by Terence Feely from an original story by Avengers man Clemens. The Liverpool-born Feely also scripted 7 other episodes in the show.

'Kiss me and die' is well-regarded by fans and in the episode Jenny portrayed the oddly-named Dominie Lanceford alongside Oscar-winning actor George Chakiris (who in recent years has since turned his hand to jewellery designing).

Dominie resides in a spruce country house near a picturesque village and stirs up all kinds of trouble after becoming emotionally involved with a visiting American. The brother of whom comes to the area to investigate his siblings mysterious disappearance. In turn, he too becomes drawn to Ms.Lanceford (Jenny) as things begin to turn nasty all about.

The makers of Thriller utilized 16mm film stock for external scenes and videotape for all interiors, a visual idiosyncrasy not welcomed by all viewers at the time or since. Stories from the series were repeated into the early-1980s and also the mid-1990s until a definitive box set containing all the episodes was released on DVD in 2005. Thriller was made in Britain for Lew Grade's Incorporated Television Company (ITC), who also presented Jenny's 1976 film The Eagle has Landed as well as The Man in the Iron Mask.

A Legacy (1975) 50 mins

Shown in March of that year, little information is available about this 5 episode television series within which Jenny was cast as Melanie Merz. It was written for the small screen by Robert Mullen from a 1956 novel by Sybille Bedford. Her most well-known work, it detailed the life of her family and another, in Germany, when the Kaiser ruled. This 'elegant, insightful work' as Peter Vansittort described it in her obituary (Guardian, 21/12/2006) saw its small-screen version star Irene Handl, Claire Bloom and Angela Pleasance.

Critical comments:

'A wonderful piece of TV well-worth reviving.' (Ref: Nick Suess, Imdb.co.uk)

Shadows (1975) 30 mins

This was an anthology series of spooky tales made for children by Thames Television. Created back in 1968 they produced some great shows including The Sweeney, Man about the House and Minder.

Jenny can be seen in 'The Waiting Room' episode, which was the fourth in the first series, and screened in September 1975.

Playing Sue in amongst a small cast, this particular story was written by Jon Watkins, who also worked on Terry & June and Father, Dear Father. Two further series followed and a tie-in paperback was also released in 1979.

The Six Million Dollar Man (1977) 60 mins

An American Werewolf in London creator John Landis had acted in episode of this series in 1974 prior to Jenny appearing in 2 episodes in 1977 Cast as a scientist called Russell across both episodes titled 'Deadly Countdown'. Originally shown on the ABC network in America more than a hundred episodes were made between 1974-8. Ms Agutter could be seen next to Steve Austin (the splendid Lee Majors) in shows that were screened at the end of September 1977.

By the time she acted in this, The Six Million Dollar Man was in to its fifth season and numbered 80 episodes.

Running at an hour for each story, the basic premise saw the rebuilding of Steve Austin (Majors whose wife Farah Fawcett had appeared with Jenny in the sci-fi film Logan's Run, the previous year) by military experts. Covertly done, he became the recipient of super-strength body parts that allowed him to run at a vast speed and jump high into the air! Inspired by an actual NASA man and former pilot, the show proved a great telly success globally. So much so that various merchandising products were produced. Returning to Jenny's involvement; the plotline for Deadly Countdown found the daughter of Steve's pal being kidnapped and blackmailed into eliminating his friend Mr. Austin. That fails and we learn of the reasons behind the act as Steve sets off to rescue the youngsters.

School Play - BBC 2 Playhouse (1979) 75 mins

Not to be confused with the classic BBC children's show, this telly feature was shown in November 1979 with Jenny filling the role of Miss P. Jackson. A sterling cast found the lovely actress once again working with a succession of co-stars either already familiar or later becoming so: Denholm Elliott, Jeremy Clyde (The Alan Clarke Diaries) and Michael Kitchen (The Buccaneers/ The Railway Children).

Directed by James Cellan Jones, this was a quality production with its writer Frederick Raphael, who worked with Kubrick on the screenplay of Eyes Wide Shut (1999) and had previously won an Oscar for his Darling (1965) screenplay.

Concluding the entry, Tim Pigott-Smith was also in the cast and he who would go on to work Jenny in an episode of Agatha Christie: Poirot in 2006.

Mayflower : The Pilgrim's Adventure (1979) 97 mins

'The voyage that changed the course of history' Also known under the snappier title of The Voyage of the Mayflower, Jenny played Priscilla Mullens, one of the travellers aboard the famous ship as its passengers made their way to a new life in America. A War of Children (1972) director George Schaefer steered a mixed cast that included Star! (1967) actor Richard Crenna and Anthony Hopkins as Captain Jones. Schaefer died in 1979 after directing this and loads of other television productions over the course of his career. Writer James Lee Barrett had the task of re-telling the true-life story of the Assembly of pilgrims who fled persecution in Britain for a proposed fresh start far across the Atlantic. His screenplay, one of many in a lengthy CV, detailed the life experience on board the ship as they strived towards a new beginning with great endeavour.

Made specifically for the CBS network in America, Mayflower was originally shown during the 1979 'thanksgiving' holiday festivities.

Critical comments:

'Great supporting cast. Excellent costuming and believable performances all around. Pleasingly simple in its approach and production…'
(Ref: duraflex, Imdb.com)

'…95% of the film takes place on the boat (The Mayflower). If you are in the mood for something pretty simple to watch...there isn't much history to learn from this film and Anthony Hopkins doesn't give his best performance. I'd give it a C+.'
(Ref: aarti, www.imdb.com)

Beulah Land (1980) 120 mins

'An epic saga of love, war and betrayal in the Old South.' Video cover slogan.

Jenny was cast somewhat unusually as an English prostitute married to a slave wrangler in the Deep South during the American civil war. As Lizzie Corlay, it was her first significant role on U.S television in a 3 episode mini-series that was Emmy-nominated. Similarly with Brit telly counterpart of sorts, A Respected Trade, Beulah Land found its original source via a novel, 1 of 3 by Lonnie Coleman.

Directed by Harry Falk, a vastly eclectic American television director on shows like the Colbys, Magnum PI and The Doris Day Show back in the1960s. The series premiered on television in October 1980 with Michael Sarrazin and the lovely Lesley Anne Warren the leading names in this glossy, small-screen production.

Critical comments:

'The miniseries is far too melodramatic compared to its source material. Sure, there are some historical inaccuracies in the books but all in all the characters are well-thought out. The characters of Sarah, Loretta and Annabelle are surprisingly real, in my opinion, and readers really get a chance to know them because they each remain fairly prominent throughout all three novels. Each remains entirely true to her character to the last.'
(Ref: BlueShirt69, Amazon.com)

The Tragedy of Othello - The Moor of Venice (1981) 195 mins

'Let me live tonight! Kill me tomorrow!'

With a line like that the viewer can imagine what the rest of the mood is across the 5 acts of this Shakespearian drama. A running time of some 3 hours sees this jaunty production of arguably the most controversial Shakespeare play, finding Jenny in the role of Desdemona.

A pale skinned appearance, all bodiced-up (at one stage she has to ask her maid to 'unpin me' prior to taking to her bed) fulfils an initially restrained role before the plot really ignites from Act III onwards. With her hair the longest that I have seen it, at waist-length, she is complimented by booming American actor William Marshall in the title role and Jenny's Dominique is Dead associate, the real star of the production, Ron Moody as Iago.

As 'gentle mistress' Desdemona, she is first seen looking down from a window as the story opens. Jenny and William convey the emotions between the couple admirably as events conspire to dupe Othello (Marshall) into believing that his wife has cuckold him. Upon hearing news of the so-called deceit, the effect proves both tremendous and tragic for each of them.

The 'devil' declares her innocence and disbelief at being seen as a perpetrator of such an abhorrent deed but that does not prevent her powerful husband from attacking her. Othello strangles her in their bed and consequently, overcome with grief and guilt, he commits suicide next to her upon discovering the actual truth.

Oddly, Jenny is listed in the end credits as 'Jennifer A.Aguter' a moniker that I had not seen before. Of course, we know that her full name is Jennifer Ann Agutter but why the overt formality?

Directed by Franklin Melton, Othello was originally written in c.1603-4 and was first performed in April 1610 at the famous Globe theatre in London. Ben 'Silas Marner' Kingsley played the title role in the 1985 Royal Shakespeare theatre production and continued the long line of notable actors. Zoe Wanamaker, star of drama series Love Hurts; within which Jenny made two appearances, also acted in a small-screen version. Released on more than one occasion on video and DVD, the January 2001 'Kultur' label is said to have an introduction from Jenny. She also furnished similar duties on the 1983 Revelation Films video release of Antony and Cleopatra.

The Jenny version is not to be confused with the Anthony Hopkins adaptation which was made for the BBC and released in the same year.

Critical comments:

'The guy who played Othello was good. Jessica from Logan's Run, always hot. But Iago was just as powerful a character as he should or could be. Not the best production ever, but stayed closer to the play then Orson Welles or Kenneth Brannagh versions.' (Ref: http://www.sukip.com)

A Dream of Alice (1982) unknown mins

This was a musical version of scenes from Alice in Wonderland, with material written by Benny Green. The programme was made to commemorate the 150th anniversary of Lewis Carroll with Jenny finding herself in amongst a cast which included Michael Horden, John Clive and Nyree Dawn Porter.

This Office Life (1984) unknown mins

Jenny starred as Pam in this Keith Waterhouse-created BBC production that was shown originally back in December '84. It was directed by former actor Ian Keill and based upon the original Waterhouse novel 'Office Life' published back in 1978. The late Mr Waterhouse had written many comedy novels and for people of a certain age, he is most fondly recalled for co-writing the Worzel Gummidge television series back in the 1970s. Also in the cast list of This Office Life were Dinsdale Landen, Rosemary Leach, Roy Kinnear and Catweazle's Geoffrey Bayldon.

Love's Labour's Lost (1985) 120 mins

'I was as willing to grapple as he was to board.' Back in 1978 the BBC set about the commendable task of recording every Shakespeare play and Jenny acted in this studio-bound entry from that illustrious list (as Rosaline). Presented in January 1985, this 'playful and elaborate' 5 act production gave another 'And Jenny Agutter' screen credit. Jenny is in amongst a radiant female group of ladies led by the multi-talented Maureen Lipman, a performer of whom Jenny waxed lyrically about in a subsequent television documentary and a sparkling David Warner was also in the cast. Jenny looks scrumptious in a padded, cumbersome dress with much tongue-twisting dialogue as a 'nimble, stirring spirit.' Lots of verbal jousting ensues between the sexes with Lipman enjoying the battle and often outwitting the men. To 'mock the mock' as she puts it. Ms.Agutter looks quite beautiful here and has 2 costume changes during the course of the story.

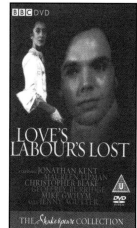

Originally, Shakespeare cast young boys in the female roles such as the one played by Jenny and early performances often took place at halls, court and courtyard's of inns. Also in a role was Geoffrey Burridge, Harry Berman in An American Werewolf in London (1981).

Magnum (1985) 60 mins

Jenny acted in 'Little Games', which was episode 12 in series/ season 5. Starring the mustachioed Tom Selleck as a Hawaii-based private detective, 162 episodes were made across an eight year period and Jenny's appearance came in amongst the 21 episodes that season.

Silas Marner - The Weaver of Raveloe (1985) 91 mins

'Miss Nancy Lammeter.
You are the glory of the county.
The crowning glory.'
Future 'Freddie' co-stars Ben Kingsley and Jenny come together in this pre-Industrial revolution-set period drama from the pen of Middlemarch author George Eliot. Although the former duo do not feature greatly together in scenes from this BBC adaptation.

It was written by Louis Marks and director Giles Foster from the original 1861 novel.

Mary Ann Evans (aka George Eliot) was born in Warwickshire and following the death of her mother took charge of the family household. In 1841 she moved with her father and subsequently stayed with him until his death in 1849. She is buried in Highgate Cemetery in north London. Kingsley shines as the initially emotionally-detached Silas and seems to be able to do any accent whatsoever and utilized this skill in the likes of Gandhi (1982) through to Sexy Beast (2000) and to the American intoned You Kill Me (2007). He and Jenny both provided their vocal talents for the ill-received animated feature Freddie as F.R.0.7, as does Freddie Jones who is also in this piece. Angela Pleasance, daughter of Donald, also has a role. The catatonic Silas finds himself bringing up an orphaned child called Eppie (played as a young adult by the terrible Patsy Kensit from teh Magic Door) who he finds outside his door one cold evening. Unbeknownst to him, her morphine-addicted mother is estranged from husband Godfrey (Patrick Rycart) one of the two sons of the local Squire. As Nancy, Jenny puts in a subtle performance in an otherwise humdrum part. Previously, Marner had been expelled from a closed religious society after mistakenly being accused of theft and moves away to spend a life working vigorously on his home weave; hence the title of the work. Silas has his life savings stolen by the wretch that is Dunstan (Jonathan Coy), the no-good son of Squire Cass (Jones) in another of those moneyed families with very little real collateral to speak of (or at least on offer to wasteful siblings). Coy, an actor that seems to have been in lots of telly series, also acted with Jenny in another show: TECX.

'Everything comes to light in the end.' Laments Godfrey (Ryecart) to his sympathetic wife (Jenny) upon his revelation that the child taken in by the weaver is actually his daughter. This plays as a very moving scene in which Eppie rejects the obvious bounties on offer to her in favour of remaining dedicated to Silas and later married to an affable young man. All in all, Silas Marner - The Weaver of Raveloe is smashing entertainment and offers a delightful performance by Mr. Kingsley. A ringlet-haired Jenny does not feature heavily in the story but we do get to enjoy seeing her in a dancing sequence at the Cass family house (prior to being proposed to by one of the brothers). The production again sees Jenny maximizing her equestrian skills: here taking charge of a horse and trap ala The Eagle has Landed.

For its Australian audience it was simply known as Silas Mariner. Location shooting took place in the picturesque Cotswolds region.

Critical comments:

'The film is rich in symbolism and imagery. Skies brood, fireplaces glow. The poorest of the poor are wealthy with love…pays close attention to period

detail, presenting clopping horses, magnificent castles, lively jigs, country church bells, and the wedding of commoners who enjoy being commoners. Carl Davis enhances the atmosphere with a music score mimicking the moods of the characters and settings. And the supporting actors undergird Kingsley's splendid performance with wonderful performances of their own.'
(Ref: Mike Cummings, All Movie Guide at Answers.com)

The Twilight Zone (1987) unknown mins

A true cult classic, this television series originally aired on American television between 1959-64. A 1983 feature film version was released with An American Werewolf in London director John Landis working with Steven Spielberg and two others in a reworking of some episodes. However, Jenny was to feature in a new colour series (episodes: Voices in the Earth & A Day in Beaumont/ The Last Defender of Camelot, 1987 & '86 respectively) which incorporated 2 or 3 stories into each of its hour-long episodes. In the first episode that Jenny worked on, her character was called Morgan Le Fa whilst in the other, it was Jacinda. The shows aired on the CBS network but did not prove to be a ratings success alas.

Love Hurts (1988) 40 mins

Created by Marks & Gran, the writing team behind Shine on Harvey Moon and Birds of a Feather,

Jenny features in 2 episodes of this excellent drama. Adam Faith and Zoe Wannamaker starred as the sometimes lovers across 30 episodes from 1992-94. Cast as Jeanette Summers, all soft, flowing hair and pearls, she played a newly-single lady with an interest in Frank (Faith) as both a friend and possible partner initially in the Tracks of my Tears episode. A radiant looking Jenny features in two scenes in the interim when Frank and Tess (Wanamaker) have split up but subsequently get back together at the series close. She returns in Cards on the Table, again seemingly heading towards a possible relationship with Frank before fate intervenes. Silly Frank is clearly still in love with Tessa and poor Jeanette (Jenny) hears all about it from him before finally giving up following his hospital dash at the end of the episode. A case of almost but not quite.

Dear John: USA (1989) 30 mins

'Oh, this really was worth the trip!'
Jenny in the American version of the John Sullivan-penned comedy series.
Written originally by the man that gave us Only Fools and Horses, Dear John was a 1980s BBC comedy series before being re-imagined for America as Dear John: USA. A completely new cast was provided with Taxi star Judd Hirsch stepping in to the lead role dealing with the characters attending a divorced persons group.
Jenny features in an excruciating episode titled The British are coming. Sullivan was a consultant for the

remake and Jenny played Sarah, sounding more Australian than English (think atypical Alison Steadman in any Mike Leigh film). She is all frilly blouse, long skirt and hair, as the sister of one of the attendees of the group. The others there spring to the latter's aid in providing a pretend husband for her visiting family who would be distressed to think that she is unmarried and with child. Unfortunately, they all turn up at her apartment without each realizing that the others are trying to fool the visitors too! Great premise but poorly executed.

Recorded before a studio audience this mistaken-identities episode is sporadically funny but plays more like a bedroom farce than anything else. Whilst Jenny is a little odd-sounding, her family members, clearly American actors, put in Dick Van Dyke accents, all different, in super o-b-v-i-o-u-s-l-y e-n-g-l-i-s-h intonations. Think the awful tones of Daphne and her mother in Fraser and you have it about right. Lila Kaye, the barmaid at the creepy pub in An American Werewolf in London (1981) also features.

The Equalizer (1989) 60 mins

'The baddest man in the whole damn town.' DVD cover slogan.

Although not regarded as much of a success in Britain when it first came out, The Equalizer was very well-received in America and ran for 4 series across 1985-89.

Forever remembered for his roles in the small-screen series Callan and The Wicker Man (1973) the dependable British actor Edward Woodward starred as the man of the title. Aka Robert McCall, he was a former espionage operative turned private investigator/ vigilante helping those that needed it via an ad in the classifieds: 'Got a problem? Odds against you? Call the Equalizer' ran the message from the smartly-dressed, Jag driving McCall. Jenny played in an episode from this now-cult show in February 1989 from series 4. Titled 'The Visitation' she was Dr. Lauren Demeter in what was the ninth story from that series or 'season' as the Americans like to term it. Close to 90 episodes were recorded. Jenny and Edward Woodward reconvened their working association after both being cast in the 1971 BBC production of The Cherry Orchard. He died in November 2009 and Jenny was interviewed for a news report.

Not a Penny More, Not a Penny Less (1990) 200 mins

I remember quite enjoying this mini-series when it was shown on BBC 1 via 50 minute chunks. With its adaptation by the experienced Sherman Yellen from jailbird Jeffrey Archer's debut novel, Jenny played Jill Albery, in amongst a predominantly male cast headlined by Ed Asner (TV's Lou Grant). A freshly-printed paperback was produced with a special cast-related cover but alas it did not include Jenny.

As Jill, Jenny joins together with 4 others made penniless by confidence trickster Harvey Metcalfe (Asner) in a plot to con the con artist and get their money back (hence the exact title).

For its American telly audience the episodes were shown as 2 x 120 minutes features but I think it worked more successfully in its British format.

Not a Penny More, Not a Penny Less had one of those irritatingly annoying theme tunes that even now remains in my head; it was reminiscent of celebrity quiz show Blankety Blank. Look out for Ed Begley Jr. as one of those who loses his savings. Begley was in a separate segment to Jenny in the feature film parody Amazon Women on the Moon (1987).

TECX (1990) 60 mins

Here is an ITV series that has still not been released on DVD. The first of its 13 episodes premiered in March 1990 with Jenny featuring lightly as Kate Milverton across 7 of them which were shown up until August of that same year. Tecx was the name of an international detective agency based in Brussels and run by a trio of characters. Plot lines involved stories taking the cast to Holland, France, Britain and Belgium. Not well-received by critics, Jenny associates Freddie Jones and Jonathan Coy also featured. The show was made by Central Films Production for now-defunct Central Television and received an American telly release.

Critical comments:
'...well-intentioned but uninspiring.'
(Ref: Boxtree Encyclopaedia of TV Detectives)

The Outsiders (1990) 90 mins

'All they have is all they need: each other.'
U.S television trailer for the show.
Based on characters from the 1967 novel by S. E. Hinton, the series came after the cult 1983 film of the same name directed Francis Ford Coppola. Despite healthy ratings for its U.S television premiere in March 1990 it proved to be a short-lived series. Jenny received a co-starring credit at the end of the pilot episode for her role as Maria Rogers. That feature-length show served as a sequel to the film but when the series was moved to a regular timeslot of 7 p.m, ratings quickly tailed off. After eight episodes, the Fox network cancelled The Outsiders. Its remaining four episodes aired through July and gave an early spotlight to Billy Bob Thornton.

Boon (1991) 60 mins

Jenny features as Melissa Dewar in a show titled 'Help me make it through the Night'. It was the first in the sixth series and was shown on ITV in September 1991. The basic premise being that her husband thinks she is having an affair and employs Ken Boon (the lugubrious Michael Elphick) to investigate matters further.

The Good Guys (1992) 60 mins

This was an excellent ITV comedy drama series which combined the celebrated telly names of Keith Barron and Nigel Havers. Both are called Guy hence the title and join together in a show created especially for them. Jenny acted in the third episode of series I called 'The McQuarrie Treasure', as a character unsympathetically called Grizel. The series was introduced in January 1992 and saw its final appearance in the following February. It seems that The Good Guys has never received a DVD release and does not appear to have been repeated on the channel either. Keith Barron also appeared alongside Jenny in an episode of the enjoyable comedy drama New Tricks in 2005.

Dream On (1992) 30 mins

Over a hundred, half hour episodes were recorded of this adult-themed comedy detailing the life of Martin Tupper (Brian Benben), a divorced book editor living in New York City. Jenny featured in the story 'No Deposit, No Return' which was the 51st episode; 1 of 25 from its third and final series. Partly shown by Channel 4, Dream On was devised by An American Werewolf in London creator John Landis who had the idea to utilize the innumerable back catalogue of old telly shows held by Universal studios. He brought in future *Friends* creators Crane and Kauffman to devise a structure and Dream On was the result.

It ran from 1990-96 and focussed upon Martin, whose formative years were spent in front of the goggle box which subsequently provide him with all his learnt life skills coming via clips of old black and white shows to express his feelings and views. A similar idea had been used in the Steve Martin film Dead Men Don't Wear Plaid (1982). Landis directed many episodes and was able to indulge in his proclivity for large breasts: see Werewolf or Into the Night (1985) for further examples. The man behind Michael Jackson's seminal music video Thriller did not, however, direct the Jenny episode which aired on American TV in October 1992 where she played a woman called Ellen. A Dream On box set containing series I & II is now available on DVD but at the time of writing, series III is not.

Red Dwarf (1993) 30 mins

'Isn't she gorgeous?'
Robert Llewellyn (Kryten in the series)
Jenny puts in a very small cameo in the opening episode of series 6 of this hugely funny comedy sci-fi show that is much-loved by its legion of dedicated fans.
Working on her scenes across a day's filming at what was to become the Tate Modern in London, she has fun as the baddie in the story and was said to be thrilled at appearing on the show.
For the uninitiated, Red Dwarf is the ship inhabited by Lister, Rimmer, Kryten and Cat who

travel the universe and get into all kinds of trouble in a more-humorous variation of Star Trek. Written in the form of 30-minute episodes, creators Rob Grant and Doug Naylor saw their show win a comedy award in 1994 for one of the episodes in this series. Titled Psirens, Jenny's involvement was in this opening episode in a very strong series shown on the BBC in October 1993. A 'Psiren' is able to take the life form of something appertaining to its victim and then alters the victim's perception telepathically before sucking their victim's brain out through a straw! Watching the show is much more enjoyable than trying to describe its plot. Wearing thigh length boots and a shiny green top Jenny appears as the bizarrely-coiffured Professor Mamet, Kryten's creator, but who is clearly not what she seems. She is only in the last five minutes prior to getting squished by a cubic Kryten (see it to understand) and that's your lot. A great appearance.

As the droid Kryten, Llewellyn shared a makeshift dressing room with Jenny whilst filming and reveals this in the cast commentary featured in the DVD box set of Series 6. He is ribbed by his fellow actors upon disclosing that whilst having intricate facial make-up administered Jenny had to get changed in the same room and asked him not to look. He did the gentlemanly thing but was teased by the others who said he should have sneaked a peek!

The Animated Shakespeare - A Winter's Tale (1994) 27 mins

'If this be magic, let it be an act lawful as eating.' Jenny offered her charismatic vocal talents to this pan-European (Welsh/ Russian) series made for television. Each being about 30 minutes in duration, A Winter's Tale was included in the comedy section alongside Twelfth Night, As You like It and A Midsummer Night's Dream. In all, 12 were made and originally shown on BBC 2 in December 1994. All were adapted by Leon Garfield, a respected Shakespearian scholar with this entry utilising plasticine animation whilst 1 or 2 others used drawn animation. Each works well in bringing Shakespeare to an audience perhaps hesitant at watching the usual three-hour-bore productions of before. Although in their defence, The Tragedy of Othello - The Moor of Venice proves a very rewarding watch.

A Winter's Tale is not the most well-known of the bard's work but it is well told. The animation here has a distinctive European feel: graceful but quite other-worldly. Jenny plays Hermione, 'the good Queen' to another mistakenly-cuckold husband, so often a plot device incorporated by Shakespeare. Some terrible events occur and result in the Queen being found guilty of 'high treason' and dying soon after of a broken heart before returning as a spirit to guide her young children.

At the story close, her lustrous statue is presented to the King who is so overwhelmed at its life-like qualities that a moment later it magically comes to life. All proves to be well again in a lovely-looking piece with Michael Kitchen, father from the 2000 telly production of The Railway Children, also providing his voice to the project.

The ideas presented in the project proved a success and the series won 2 American Emmy awards.

Critical Comments:

'It's a kind of Shakespeare's Greatest Hits: all the best-known lines and key action with narrators filling in the gaps.'

(Ref: R Mackie, Guardian).

Romeo and Juliet (1994) 81 mins

'Alack the day, she's dead, she's dead, she's dead!'
(Act IV, scene 5)

Jenny is Lady Capulet in this small-screen adaptation by telly writer/ actor Grant Cathro of the most well-known Shakespearian tragedy/ love story.

With a running time of some 81 minutes, she had Bergerac star John Nettles (Jenny would later make an appearance in his Midsommer Murders series) as her husband Lord Capulet, in a tale that has been filmed many times before and since this version. Jonathan Firth, who is also in this had previously provided his vocal talents, alongside Jenny, in The Animated Shakespeare interpretation of A Winter's Tale. Jenny's character was the mother of the tragic Juliet and of whose husband is embedded in a feud with the Montagu family.

Heartbeat (1994 & 1996) 60 mins

'Being good is always easy…'

Originally airing on ITV in 1992, this popular 1960s-set drama continued on with cast changes not preventing it reaching close to 300 episodes. Jenny can be seen in two stories as Susannah Temple-Richards: in Fair Game & The Best Laid Plans. In the first, a duplicitous Jenny is seen on screen immediately, chucking bails of hay around with her intentions clearly set firmly on some extra-marital shenanigans with a young man. Looking very contemporary with longer hair complimenting her features, her character ends up being taken away in the back of a police car as the episode concludes. Insipid wooden top Nick Berry sets out to investigate the accidental death of her husband and it is revealed that she unintentionally proves responsible for his death via a hunting accident. Regrettably, this being the country, that so-called sport proves popular amongst the big wigs of the village and Jenny is seen in full riding regalia (I have to concede that she looks absolutely sensational in bowler hat, white gloves and suit). Niamh Cusack, Jenny's screen daughter in telly drama 4:50 from Paddington, shares a moment on screen here as does Equus co-star Peter Finch in the same episode. Ms. Cusack acted across nearly fifty episodes in the early-1990s whilst Spooks star Firth furnished seven episodes in 1994 as a doctor at the same practice as her. Simon Ward from I Start Counting and Dominique is Dead also appeared in an episode but not with Jenny alas. He was great in The Four Feathers (1977) which also starred The Survivor man Robert Powell. Simon also had a role in The Monster Club. Derek Fowlds from East of Sudan (1964) acted in more than 300 episodes of this family-friendly series which features classic music from the period. The storywriters had the clever idea of re-introducing Susannah (Jenny) in a later episode titled The Best Laid Plans continuing her story after being released from prison for the manslaughter of her lush of a husband previously. She comes into the plot soon on in and looks resplendent with a Cilla Black-type bob hairstyle. Seeking to rebuild her life in a more modest manner alas for her (and somewhat predictably for the viewer) a former prison lag returns to see 'Suze' and immediately begins to manipulate her. Things do not go well and Jenny ends up being bound and gagged in the back of a car before being rescued by the police. No Niamh Cusack in this episode as she had already left the series. Maybe not such a dynamic episode as the 1994 one, the 1996 tale is still professionally executed and an easy watch for what was a Sunday evening telly presentation on ITV 1. Heartbeat was cancelled in January 2009.

The All New Alexei Sayle Show (1995) 30 mins

Jenny appears as a scientist in a spoof segment of this comedy sketch show which was the fourth outing for the Liverpudlian stand-up. She featured alongside Peter Capaldi in a sci-fi parody called 'Drunk in Time'. Sayle, now a novelist, was assisted by future Father Ted creators Graham Linehan and Arthur Matthews to script this comedy sequel to his 'Stuff' series.

Shown on BBC2 between January 1994 and July1995, The All New Alexei Sayle Show won a prestigious Bronze Rose of Montreux award in 1995 and an American Emmy. Jenny's episode was shown in 1995 and she had already featured in a similar parody, also on the same channel, Red Dwarf, back in 1993.

The Buccaneers (1995) 220 mins

Adapted from the final, uncompleted novel by American author Edith Wharton, this UK produced mini-series is not to be confused with the 1950s swashbuckling serial starring Robert Shaw. Ms.Wharton was the first woman to win the Pulitzer Prize in 1921 for The Age of Innocence (made in to a film by Martin Scorsese in 1993). Written back in 1938, the novel was later completed by Marion Mainwaring. The Buccaneers was shown in February 1995. Totalling 5 episodes at 55 minutes each, Jenny features in 4 of them as Idina Hatton. Her Railway Children husband Michael Kitchen, effective as the father in the 2000 television adaptation was also in this. Directed by Philip Saville, a London-born actor, writer and director the screenplay was written by experienced telly scribe Maggie Wadey. Not surprisingly, the series won a BAFTA for Best Costume design.

Critical comments:

'Splendid entertainment and with all confidence I can truly say that this film is one of closest films to reach to perfection that I have ever seen.' (REF: Thornfield2, Imdbd.com).

Murder She Wrote (1996) 60 mins

The infuriatingly irritable Jessica Fletcher as played here by Bedknobs and Broomsticks actress Angela Landsbury starred in numerous telly adventures as a middle-aged novelist prone to solving various crimes. Ala Miss Marple or Poirot, she succeeded in annoying viewers across 1984-96 and perennial afternoon repeats ever since. Incredibly enough, more than 200 episodes were filmed and were first shown on Brit TV in 1985.

Jenny played a character called Margo Claymore in One White Rose for Death; episode 4 (of 22) in the third series. It finds Jessica being held hostage in amongst a hot pot of political espionage and defection. Jenny associates Ron Moody and Judy Geeson acted in the same episode together of this series and The Survivor helmer David Hemmings directed a single episode in 1987.

And The Beat Goes On (1996) 52 mins

'For god's sake, we're not some moonstruck teenagers anymore.'

Jenny starred as Connie Spencer in this amiable Channel 4 drama which ran across 8 episodes. Stephen Moore co-stars in a serial about two vastly opposing, Liverpool-based families as the swinging 1960s comes in to being. One brood being working class whilst the other distinctly middle class: you can guess which one Ms.Agutter belonged too.

Written, created by and starring a number of faces from behind and in front of the camera, from the now-defunct soap Brookside, And The Beat Goes On has clear echoes of the burgeoning 'Liverpool' sound championed by groups such as The Beatles & Gerry and the Pacemakers. Episodes went out on a Tuesday evening at 10pm with a handy highlights recap from the previous show and next often using Jenny.

Episode i: an establishing one which sees Jenny with super short hair and postcard shots of the Liver building at the former port. As Constance or 'Connie', Jenny's telly family consists of two mid-teens children, a borasic brother suffering for his sexual predilections (a memorable performance by Dominic Jephcott) and a husband, Nicholas that shows her little notice (Moore). Her character ends up in a private nursing home after suffering a nervous breakdown by the end of the episode.

Episode ii: with Jenny's name featuring first on the opening credits, And the Beat Goes On used a number of different directors across its storylines. Clad in that middle-class symbol of pearls, Connie is a miserable role at first with hubby heading away from his wife as his political ambitions to become a Tory M.P. place a strain on their fractious family and personal relationship. Appearances being all for politicians, Jenny is obliged to play the dutiful wife ala Jane Clark.

Episode iii: an important episode with a lot happening for Jenny's character: she gets caught shoplifting and her 'difficulties' as they are termed, cause her tremendous mental anxiety. The story ends with a distraught Connie (Jenny) tearring down a built-up street in the family car only to hit a child on the roadside.

Episode iv: a classic 'hit and run' scenario ensues as Connie confesses to her husband what happened. He offers her no emotional support and does not want her to tell the police as it will affect his career aspirations. With her fragile mental health failing even more so, he gets elected as the local M.P with the assistance of Howard (a dastardly Philip McGough), all the while his wife crumbles under the burden of her guilt.

Episode v: this particular episode opens with a literal shock for both Jenny's character and the audience: she is seen having e.c.t (electro-convulsive therapy) aka electric-shock treatment. It looks as brutal as it was in actuality. Post-treatment Jenny resembles the actress that is familiar to us: her hair straight and flat but still looking very pretty. Peter Firth, so captivating in Equus (1977) comes in to the series as Francis, an orderly at the nursing home involved with assisting patients such as her. They chat and seem to know each other but all is yet to be revealed.

Episode vi: 'That chap looks familiar…' offers a vague Nicholas upon seeing Francis with Connie as he pays his wife a fleeting visit. The orderly and Mrs Spencer are spending a lot of time together and it is revealed that its been more than 20 years since they've seen one another: but what is their association?

Episode vii: 'I don't deserve you…' Connie and Francis kiss passionately as the truth of their teenage relationship is made evident via a sojourn to the seaside at nearby New Brighton. When she was Connie Fairbrother, Jenny's character fell pregnant as an 18-year-old but was forced to give the baby up for adoption. Meanwhile Francis was swiftly pushed away by the scoffing family and not seen again until all these years later. Her seemingly loveless marriage is further decaying.

Episode viii: possibly the strongest story of all, Connie returns home to discover the police are still investigating the death of the child. She and Francis meet up once more at New Brighton where she confesses her involvement in the accident. He later turns up at the family home and says that he still wants them to build a new life together. Despite confessing that he has never stopped loving her, events transpire to force her confession about the damaged car to the police quiz them about. Astonishingly, Moore's character confesses to the deed as well as her!

All the while Francis is waiting at the train station for her to join him in their proposed new life. Here the plot strands are tied up with members of the other family also at the station, independently. The train departs with a dejected Francis still on the platform. 'Why?' asks Jenny to her husband after his unexpected sacrifice. 'Because I love you.' Comes his response. Very entertaining stuff.

September (1996) 185 mins

'A drama of intrigue and suspicion, set in the isolated world of the Scottish Highlands.'
DVD strap line.

Also known as 'Rosemund Pilcher - September' for its German audience (where her work is very popular and has received many adaptations).

Jenny is billed in a supporting role as Lady Isobel Balmerino, in this two-parter written by Lee Langley. Mostly fondly remembered for her novel The Shell Seekers, the 1990 novel September was Ms.Pilcher's second book to be reworked for film/ television and the film enjoyed a not unsubstantial $7.5 million budget.

Caught in a complicated, non-tactile marriage with Lord Archie (a Churchillian-sounding Edward Fox) she is seen within the first five minutes driving a people carrier. The couple may well be titled but life for them is proving hard even though they live alongside the affluent likes of Virginia McKenna and a Rolls-Royce driving Michael York.

So they begrudgingly take in tourists to bring in much-needed funds.

Jenny looks dapper in a floppy hat in this pan-European production which commenced shooting in August 1994 and aired on UK television exactly 4 years later. Titled September as much of the key plot moments occur in that month, the piece is set in the Scottish Highlands but was actually shot in Ireland. Similarly, Jenny's BBC drama series The Invisibles was also filmed in Ireland (doubling for Cornwall).

Directed by Colin Bucksey, September offered the scrumcious Jacqueline Bisset a prime role as a family figure returning home some twenty years after her mysterious departure. As Pandora, Ms.Bisset's character proves a positive effect upon her troubled brother (Fox) and his relationship with his wife (Jenny) and also brings her own troubles to a very busy plotline. The film reunited Logan's Run leads Michael York (looking very well preserved) and Jenny Agutter almost thirty years after that film. They do appear on screen together but only interact in relation to others. Alas they share no dialogue within a production that is very well done with a literary script.

As a Falklands veteran, Fox's interpretation of Archie proves grating or initially it does. But as the story progresses he becomes more likeable.

However, there seems to be so many strands to the storyline that the film-makers do not dwell too long upon any given relationship. Nonetheless, Jenny does have her moment in this entertaining two-parter with a marvellous cast looking at ease.

She has a nude scene but this time as a precursor to some lovely intimacy between the couple (although their on-screen kissing proves a little over-powering for the viewer: watch it and see what you think of Fox's hungry penguin technique!). The bath tub scene is done discreetly.

Angela Pleasance, whose father Donald was in The Eagle has Landed (not sharing any screen moments with Ms Agutter though) features as Jenny and Edward's screen daughter. The two actresses had commenced a working relationship upon both appearing in Silas Mariner: The Weaver of Ravelo for a television audience back in 1985.

Critical comments:

'I really enjoyed this...It was very true to the book, which is unusual these days. The cast consists of some of Britain's tried and true actors, a factor that made it all the more enjoyable.'
(Ref: Leonie Ganivet, amazon.com)

'On its own, it is quite a respectable movie with much to offer.'
(Ref: bookloversfriend, Amazon.com)

'You'll watch it for the stars, but it plays like a day-time soap. The acting is good most of the time (these people are real pros), but key moments are played so artificially that your mind starts to wander.' (Ref: Imdb.com)

'While several of the major actors walk through their roles with no strain, little gems of acting appear in the lesser roles, like the dotty woman, and the little boy who plays the son.'
(Ref: Barbara Harrelson, Amazon.com)

Bramwell (1998) 120 mins

'A sort of Boer War version of E.R'
Journalist Alice Wooley.

Three series of this Victorian medical drama were made for ITV in the mid-1990s before it returned in 1998. Jenny features in both of the lengthy episodes contained within the fourth series and the programmes are available on an American Region 1 DVDs (viewable on multi-region players).

Its principal cast was lead by Jemma Redgrave, David Calder and Robert Hardy in a period costume drama set in the late 19th century. Redgrave plays Eleanor Bramwell, a pioneering doctor struggling to find her place in society and often coming in to conflict with her father Robert (Calder).

Bramwell was created by Lucy Gannon, who also devised Soldier, Soldier. Jenny acted in 2 episodes: 1) 'Loose Women' - shown in June '98 and 2) 'Our Brave Boys', also screened that month. With each feature-length episode running for 2 hours, Jenny played Mrs Bruce across both. The story therein is another traumatic trial for the young female doctor in the heart of the old East End of London.

Jenny got the role thanks to her son suggesting it to series director Paul Unwin that she would be great for it. Suitably impressed, he agreed.

Critical comments:

'Bramwell is a simply brilliant series. Jemma Redgrave was very believable as Dr. Bramwell. The show has great storylines and was extremely well-researched. It is British filmmaking at its best.'
(Ref: Meryl Heasman, PBS.org)

A Respectable Trade (1998) 60 minutes x 4

With a title reeking of irony, the Kenya-born Philippa Gregory novel was made in to a BBC mini-series in association with the Nine Network Australia and Irish Screen. Airing on television in April 1988, Ms.Gregory, a somewhat prolific author of historical pieces, also created the screenplay for the small-screen adaptation directed by seasoned telly helmer Suri Krishnamma. New Tricks actor Warren Clarke receives top billing alongside an ashen Anna Massey (from Jenny's Sweet William film). The two play the Cole siblings whose main source of income is in the trading of human beings brought over from Africa via long, arduous journeys where frequently many lives are lost.

Ms.Agutter is Lady Scott, wife of Lord Scott (Simon Williams), during a period in the 18th century wherein status, class and the knowing of ones place was paramount. Alas, Frances (Emma Fielding) fails to adhere to such rigidity and finds herself willingly agreeing to be palmed off to Josiah (Clarke) via her uncle (Williams). Frances wishes to be a dutiful wife but soon realises that her seemingly affable new husband has his own demands upon her time and effort. She is required to be a sort of governess to teach the 'savages' English and good manners so that they can be sold off to members of the upper classes as service staff. Ms Fielding's character does a lot more than that and soon becomes embroiled in a physical relationship with one of the slaves, Mehru (Ariyon Bakare), with whom she falls pregnant.

Jenny is not billed in the opening credits and her appearances are mainly brief. For example the first time she is seen is when looking through a telescope in the grounds of the sumptuous Scott estate as their niece approaches. In addition, looking very appealing in a full-length dress and heavy set curls within her shoulder-length hair, she is glimpsed in the background of a subsequent scene. Following this, with a cast all costumed-up in wigs and silks (Simon Williams looking born for this kind of no-nonsense role as guardian to the young Francis) Jenny features at the wedding ceremony of the youngster in another hefty gown which hides her legs completely. A Respectable Trade allows Jenny to wear a number of cowboy-like, curved-edged headwear which she carries off with great aplomb (think Dick Turpin meets kiss-me-quick). Her character at no time steps away from the formalities of good behaviour equally acknowledged and adhered to by most of the characters in this story which builds to quite an affecting conclusion.

Jenny acts in a brief scene with Anna Massey, with the latter looking terribly pale throughout the production. The Jenny association was further enhanced by Simon Williams who with her, provided the narration to an audio presentation of Daphne Du Maurier's Rebbeca for the Talking Classics label. Williams also acted in telly comedy Agony with Maureen Lipman (whom Jenny had worked with in a Shakespearian production) and her Number One, Longing. Number Two, Regret co-star Jeremy Bulloch.

Returning to the story, many people such as the Coles had a vested interest against the rising support for the abolition of slavery and during the tale, the 'African trade' as it was known, continued on. It would not be until a further two decades from when A Respectable Trade was set, 1807, that the trade was made illegal in the UK but still it crept on. Thankfully, with the 1833 Slavery Act all such immoral trading was finally abolished (not before many high-standing individuals were compensated for their financial losses).

Warren Clarke's portrayal of 'a man of average integrity' initially works well but this is not one of his most restrained performances in my opinion. It is Emma Fielding as the sprightly Francis who steals the production whilst Jenny looks positively regal throughout in a minor supporting presence. Both Richard Briers and Ralph Brown are also noteworthy in vastly differing moral standpoints through their roles too.

Jenny narrated the audio book which accompanied the novel, released by Harper Collins to great applause: 'Philippa Gregory's historical storytelling skills are brought vividly to life by Jenny Agutter.' Offered Choice magazine in March 1998. The mini-series was Bafta-nominated and was also the recipient of a best drama American film award in 1999.

Critical comments:

'Offers a historical insight into the stirrings of the abolitionist movement. It is a compelling film.' (Ref: 'By the book', the Knowledge Network).

The Railway Children (2000) 108 mins

'I just rediscovered that there is such longevity to that story.'

Jenny after returning to Britain after nearly two decades away in America in the late-1980s.

She has noted that some fans of the Railway Children in all its various guises were shocked to see in this new, small-screen version Jenny cast in the role of mother (as played by Dinah Sheridan in the 1970 film). She was delighted to return and expressed her delight at the rarity of being able to play your own screen mother.

However, this genteel re-interpretation of Edith Nesbit's book is nowhere near as affecting as the seminal Lionel Jeffries film. Filmed in October 1999 on the Bluebell Railway line, Sussex, this interpretation of The Railway Children aired on ITV at Easter 2000.

As we are all pretty familiar with the film version let's mention the differences inherent with this Simon Nye-scripted adaptation for Carlton TV.

1) Jenny's voice-over narration is missing - see point 12 for a further explanation.

2) She plays the role of her mother instead of Roberta who is portrayed here by Jemima Ropper.

3) Nesbit is clearly very fond of Roberta in the book and speaks directly to the reader to reiterate this. The novel has a scene where mother (Jenny) asks her daughter to be careful and not play on the railway tracks. The youngster throws the query back that she believed that her mother did the same when she was a girl. It's a bizarre scene as Jenny has a glint in her eye that almost comes across as an in-joke: she of course did play on the line but in the film and previous versions as the lovely Bobbie!

4) Doctor Forrest (David Bamber), as the local GP is nowhere near as odd as the one seen in the film. I always found him most un-nerving; take the scene where Bobbie says that she has never seen a grown man cry and his response is that he does it all the time. In the telly re-make, that line is not included and the G.P. barely features.

5) 'We're trying to be more faithful to the original novel,' offered producer Charles Elton, 'for example, we're including the canal scenes from the book, and also the scene where Bobbie gets trapped on the engine…' Reading the book, the children have an altercation with workers on the bargee (boat) and also when a baby on board is rescued from a fire by Peter. However, this does not feature in the film or the late-1960s television adaptation with Jenny in.

6) East Sussex locations replace the original Yorkshire ones so effectively incorporated in the Jeffries film. Horsted Keynes station features as the main station familiar to the children. Sharpthorne tunnel was used for the paper chase.

7) For the Carlton version, a stretch of line-side fencing was removed and a wooden one temporarily positioned for the children to sit on as they wave to passing trains below.

8) Sir Richard Attenborough, making his television debut, with an understated performance as the old gentleman has a beard but in the novel the character is clean shaven.

9) The Bluebell's SECR C-class No.592 features as the 'The Green Dragon.' And the Great Northern Railway Directors' Saloon, built in 1897, was utilised as the old gentleman's carriage.

10) Hard-man actor Clive Russell appears as the Station Master, a role only alluded to in the film. And screen luvvie Attenborough plays the bespectacled, old gentleman that the children repetitively turn to for help and advice. Scottish acting icon Gregor Fisher aka Rab C.Nesbitt, is cast in the Perks role, so brilliantly portrayed by Bernie Cribbins in the film.

11) Jenny's moving 'Daddy, my daddy!' moment features in this version with returning father and

Bobbie in a slightly different manner. The scene begins in slow-motion and works extremely well as the eldest child sees her father. The screen then returns to normal speed unlike the film which literally freezes frame for a second as the two embrace. This moment is a real tribute to Edith Nesbitt's writing and its emotional resonance reigns supreme.

12) Finally, the grating voice-over narration by Jenny upon her father's return to 'Three Chimneys' is removed. The dialogue where she says that the children are not wanted as the parents are given some moments together and leads her two siblings away. Here, the film makers improve upon the scene in my opinion by having the entire family embrace each other as the camera moves further and further off into the distance.

Jenny looks the part and projects her affection towards the three children perfectly and there are moments to enjoy in this shortened adaptation directed by Catherine Morshead. But it can only struggle in comparison to the film which simply cannot be bettered. Jemima Rooper, as Roberta, at least has some presence but otherwise Clare Thomas and Jack Blumenau are pretty nondescript as Phyllis & Peter, respectively.

To promote the show, Jenny was joined by cast members Lord Attenborough, Gregor Fisher, Jemima Rooper and Jack Blumenau at the London Transport Museum in April 2000. Meanwhile in May of that year, the Bluebell Railway and Edith Nesbit Society organised a 'Railway Children day' which saw Jenny and fellow cast and crew members from the latest version in attendance. The day saw more than £2k being raised for the Cystic Fibrosis Trust. Take a look at the Bluebell Railway site listed in the references section of this book and the CFT, of which Jenny is personally involved.

Spooks (2002) 60 mins

'You are a brilliant woman but…'

Known as 'MI-5' for its American audience, Spooks tells the disparate and often desperate tales of British counter terrorism operatives that infiltrate various scenarios to protect the crown. Led by Peter Firth, looking a lot like Nosferatu theses days, and Jenny as Tessa Phillips, also in a position of authority but not as senior as him.

Spooks has a prelim sequence prior to showing a main character montage which finds Jenny standing in an office: no actor credits are included only the name of the show. The programme has proved a massive success and is now into its ninth series.

A slick visual style gives crispness to a super show where the programme makers incorporate every trick that they can think in a fresh, glossy style. Despite the limits of a BBC budget, Spooks uses lots

of split screen sequences and looks terrific.
But even in an organisation as altruistic as the British intelligence service there will always be those that do opposite. In the case of Spooks, step forward Tessa (Jenny), looking resplendent in a crisp suit and emerald green once again. Although I have to say that her tight Mary Quant hairstyle does not flatter and presents an older-looking Jenny in an almost feline manner. Interviewed during her involvement in episodes across 2002-3, she described her character as an unpleasant, forthright individual within an emphasis firmly on the self-serving.

The makers of Spooks relied heavily on the kudos of actors such as Jenny of whom they could rely upon to express so much from a simple glance and Jenny provides quite a number of them in series I. Jeremy Bullock, her assistant in the puzzling film Number 1, Longing. Number 2, Regret, features in the Traitor's Gate episode, as does the ubiquitous Anthony Head. The latter appears in the same story line but not directly with Jenny. Written by Howard Brenton, who termed Tessa an 'evil queen' an interesting definition as Jenny played such a character in The Magic Door which co-starred a certain Mr.Head. The acting fraternity being a small world is obviously enhanced once again by Jenny acting alongside Peter Firth. The two also share a brief scene in an episode of Heartbeat and in Spooks they are really good together, often battling each other before a final denouement

where Jenny's Tessa is finally usurped at the close of the first series. The affable Bradford-born Firth is a main character in Spooks and became a major child star thanks to 1970s telly series Here Come the Double Deckers! Here's how he defined their working association, 'I feel I know Jenny as a best friend. That's what happens when you spend a long time naked together!'

Having turned 50 during the making of the series, Jenny plays in a most amusing scene with her married lover Nicholas Farrell in The Rose Bed Memoirs episode. It proves a revelation as the usually-guarded Tess gets to reveal more about her private life than had previously been forthcoming. Spooks is a busy watch with lots of plot strands occurring within the same storyline but it proves thrilling viewing. Jenny was a late addition to the cast and did not see all the scripts prior to accepting the role of Tessa Phillips across the six episodes in series I from 2002-2003.

Critical comments:

'…a show that catches your attention from start to finish. The story moves at a fast pace and while some of the action and the ways that things are solved are a little dramatic and unreal, it is still a great show…'
(Ref: song85/ unknown site)

Agatha Christie's Marple: 4.50 from Paddington (2004) 90 mins

'Tell them for us it's only love that matters.'

Furnished with a screenplay by actor/ writer Stephen Churchett, this ITV murder mystery series starred Geraldine McEwan as female sleuth Jane Marple. Christie first incorporated her back in an original 1930 novel and since then television and film adaptations have seen Gracie Fields, Margaret Rutherford, Helen Hayes, Angela Landsbury, Joan Hickson and Ms. McEwan in the leading role.

Best-remembered for her role in Mapp & Lucia, the actress infuses her interpretation as the female Poirot with much humour. Jenny is seen ever so briefly in this adaptation (originally made into a film back in 1962 after publication back in 1957). The story opens with a dying Agnes Crackenthorpe (Jenny) on her deathbed before passing away within the first two minutes of the telly film.

Christie's story is very well constructed and advances a decade before continuing thereon with murder and skulduggery abounding at Rutherford hall, the family pile. Jenny is not seen again other than by way of a momentary flashback via the thoughts of her family or in the portrait seen on the desk of her husband's study. This 4.50 from Paddington includes one of the most instantly recognizable Christie

moments within which the plot hinges and is cleverly investigated by the owl-like Miss Marple. Originally titled 4.52 from Paddington, it was changed just prior to publication as a novel. A lavish adaptation, the popular series also featured Griff Rhys Jones, Niamh Cusack and John Hannah in amongst this '4.50': a journey well-worth taking. It is is included on a 4 episode DVD box set released by ITV in 2005.

The Alan Clarke Diaries (2004) 174 mins

'The best human being in the entire world.' Mr.Clark's description of his wife Jane, as portrayed by Jenny in the mini-series.

This BBC re-imagining of the collected diaries of former maverick M.P Alan Clark proves a real blast from the 1980s/ early-1990s past back when the Labour party proved un-electable. From the vaulting ambition clasped with compulsion from the very start Clark, was keen to become a government minister and not languish amongst the back benchers in the House of Commons.

John Hurt effectively steps into his expensive shoes quite perfectly and his voice-over narration works well in this six-part serialization of the Tory's 'In Power' and 'Last Diaries' publications. Both provide rich pickings for writer/director Jon Jones. The series includes various footage from the BBC's political flagship show Question Time, the miner's strike and news headlines which remind the audience of the often tumultuous times being reacted to on screen from those directly involved on the front line.

With dark brown hair and unflattering heavy fringe, Jenny is winningly cast as Alan's dutiful wife, 'darling Jane'. Intermittently seen in the background either on the campaign trail or at the stately pile that they couple call home, she soon reveals herself as the lynchpin in the Clark machine. Indeed, upon looking back, the M.P spends most of his time lambasting himself for leaving her and his home whilst off working and conducting extra-marital affairs. To this matter he freely admits to being 'culpably weak' but as Jane, Jenny projects a dignified stance to her perpetual hurt and embarrassment whenever Alan's latest gaffe or trieste is revealed.

Jenny is not seen predominantly in this telling of Clark's rise and fall at Westminster but she succeeds in presenting Jane as a strong, sensitive woman with a mutually pronounced love for her partner. His obligatory political stance may not be

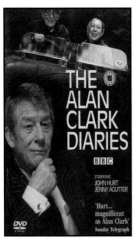

to everyone's taste and the on-screen Clark comes across as a bit of a cad, but an affable one. And you have to gasp at the gall of possibly the only man apart from Dennis, to find Mrs. Thatcher attractive. Director and scriptwriter won the 2nd Annual Directors Guild of Great Britain (DGGB) Award in 2005 for episode twowhich was titled 'The Lady'. Critical comments:

'…gripping television…It's hard to imagine a better adaptation from page to screen.'
(Ref: The Independent on Sunday)

The Inspector Lynley Mysteries (2004)
90 mins

There is a lot to like about this detective drama serial with its initial story lines taken from the 11 or so novels of American author Elizabeth Gregory. Set in Oxford and London, Jenny comes into what transpires to be an unsavoury story involving the sale of a baby, the repercussions of which becomes more and more complicated as this 90 minute drama unravels. She is cast as Jemma Sanderson, a former model and now co-host of an exclusive members-only club with her husband. A murder count of 4 is weaved into the plot written by Ann Marie di Mambo but her screenplay does not feature Jenny's elegant character much. Although, when she is seen mingling with clients she looks ravishing especially in a sleeveless dress.

Initially presented on BBC 1 from 2001 onwards, Nathaniel Parker starred as the upper crust 8th Earl of Asherton aka D.I Lynley. Jenny played in the episode 'A Cry for Justice', which was the third show in series III. The programme, one of 4 in that series, aired 18th March 2004. Some 23 have been filmed in all thus far.

Agatha Christie's Poirot (2005) 90 mins

'You've killed what?'

For some people watching a feature-length episode of another in a long litany of Agatha Christie 'whodunits' would be considered a task. What with all its plumy-voiced actors and self-confessed 'greatest detective in the world' of the little Belgian know-all Hercules Poirot proving an unappetizing small-screen morsel. However, 1 of 4 Poirot stories reworked by Guy Andrews, this one being sourced from the Christie novel Taken at the Flood (1948) is a fabulously enjoyable, well-woven tale.

A superb cast runs through an every day story involving deceit, greed, love, lust and murder which is all suitably tidied-up by Monsieur Poirot (David Suchet) and makes for delightful viewing. It was directed by Andy Wilson, whose work had also previously involved Jenny in episodes of Spooks (both 2002) and the Miss Marple telly film 4.50 From Paddington (2004). Jenny's appearance is in episode 4 of the tenth series which had begun in 1989 and continues to be made in 2009. More than 60 outings have been presented by ITV. In Taken at the Flood; Jenny co-stars as Adela Marchmont, all lovely short hair curled at the ends in this 1930s set drama (all the ITV shows are based in this decade although the original novels cover a much broader period). Her bolshie sister is played with some relish by the inimitable Celia Imrie whilst the dearly-departed Elizabeth Spriggs fills the familial Christie octogenarian role that proves to be a useful witness to a nasty murder.

This episode has all the hallmarks of a typical Christie tale; a nasty and conniving scoundrel (Elliot Cowen), beautiful young ladies (Eva Birthistle & Amanda Douge) and seemingly dependable sorts such as Jenny associate Tim Piggott-Smith.

Ms.Agutter's character comes in and out of the narrative and only has a little involvement in the story but what she does do is an impeccable job as do all the cast.

With his little upturned, slug-like moustache ala Chaplin in Monsieur Verdoux (1947) Suchet brings much humour and even a dash of pathos in this entry in the long-running series as the dapper detective. He and Jenny worked together again in 2008 on the feature film Act of God.

A mega DVD box set containing 57 episodes is now available on the ITV label. Jenny was interviewed for a television documentary 'The Agatha Christie Code' also screened in 2005.

New Tricks (2005) 60 mins

Jenny made a guest appearance in the opening episode of series two of this excellent investigative drama series. The BBC brought together a first rate cast of familiar telly names including James Bolam, Dennis Waterman, Alun Armstrong and holding them all together as Superintendent

Pullman is Amanda Redman.

In Jenny's untitled appearance, written by series co-creator Roy Mitchell, there is much humour in a sharp script involving the re-opening of a seedy1980s murder case for the U.C.O.S (Unsolved Crimes and Open Cases Squad). From the very start it is clear that Yvonne (Jenny) has something to hide from the trio of former detectives brought out of retirement to attempt to resolve unsolved such as the one involving her husband. They set about interviewing those connected in an attempt to re-interpret the case and consequently speak with Mrs Barrie (Jenny). Indeed, thanks to their clever team work, her moment of revelation comes towards the close of the story. Cleverly manipulated into revealing the tearful truth of her husband's last moments, Jenny takes centre stage in a marvellously crafted scene at a multi-story car park. All 5 actors are shot walking together as the truth unravels itself. It is a small moment but very well executed. An excellent Anita Dobson also features in the story. Jenny is not used greatly in New Tricks - making 4 brief appearances: initially giving a speech to present an award dedicated to her late husband and afterwards meeting the investigative team, later being interviewed by Armstrong and Waterman, and the final encounter as detailed.

New Tricks was co-created by Nigel McCrery and Mitchell, began its life as a one-off programme broadcast in March 2003. Following strong ratings being recorded, a full series was commissioned and subsequent ones followed. Guest stars have included Honor Blackman, Keith Barron, Timothy West and the omnipotent Anthony Head.

Perfectly done with a likeable cast, New Tricks is now successfully into its sixth or seventh series. Series 2 contained 8 episodes with Jenny's solitary appearance in the opening show being broadcast on BBC 1 in May 2005.

Critical comments:

'The series is a wonderfully different take on forensic, cold case storylines. The interaction between the four actors that make up the team, is hilarious and at the same time, full of great tensions and chemistry. The individual stories are original and often quirky.'

(Ref: Konstanz Alsop, Amazon.co.uk)

Diamond Geezer (2007) 90 mins

This fun little drama was a short-run series following the adventures of loveable seasoned criminal Des (David Jason), as he attempts to pull off several crimes. A feature-length pilot episode was shown in 2005 and was followed by a trio of further outings, all made for ITV: Old School Lies/ Old Gold and A Royal Affair (all 2007).

Jenny acted in the final story as the oddly-titled Vanessa Chabrol in a project which was really just a show for Jason fans looking for some light entertainment in a post-Del Boy role for the comedy man. The plot for Jenny's story focussed upon Des breaking into Buckingham Palace to swipe a large diamond before it is handed over to the Indian government. The task has to be completed prior to them realising that the jewel has been substituted for a fake. Diamond Geezer (aka Rough Diamond) is available in a 4-discs DVD box set.

The Invisibles (2008) 360 mins, series 1.

'It's a dream of a cast. And what's especially brilliant is the breadth of the talent on board. The Invisibles is an ensemble piece which means every character relies on the one next to them to give full value in terms of what the script is trying to achieve. And that means, in an ideal world, you're looking to fill every role with a heavy hitter - but in truth you seldom achieve that. This time, I think we have...'
Creator William Ivory interviewed on bbc.co.uk
Devised and partly scripted by Ivory, a writer that had previously sharpened his skills on Minder, The Invisibles is a quintessentially old-fashioned comedy drama. Jenny is third-billed in a BBC TV series predominantly following the supposed retirement of former 'crims' Maurice (Anthony Head) and Syd (Warren Clarke). Sometime Jenny co-star Mr.Head is the more sophisticated of the old team and is married to Barbara, or 'Babs' as he likes to call her (portrayed by an often shimmering Jenny looking especially pleasing in episode 3 in an orange evening dress). Forced out

of retirement to help others, the lads find that things have changed somewhat and enlist the help of old technical mate Paul Barber (Denzel from Only Fools And Horses) and Hedley (Dean Lennox Kelly) the son of their former crew member. They return to safe-cracking only this time with redeeming justifications set against a host of past adversaries, squabbles and lovers coming out of the proverbial woodwork.

The toad-like Clarke proves as watchable as ever and is a million miles away from his role in cult film A Clockwork Orange (1971). He and Jenny, as previously stated, had worked together on A Respectable Trade, another BBC series. Away from The Invisibles, Oldham-born Warren had starred in Dalziel and Pascoe and numerous series of Down to Earth.
Speaking about his part in The Invisibles, Anthony Head, forever remembered for his coffee ads, found the affable actor confessing to a crush on the screen Jenny after seeing her in all her

popular past projects. The two play well together in a marriage full of warmth and affection in a likeable series filmed in Northern Ireland (standing-in for Devon) across a shoot filmed in exceedingly cold temperatures.

'A good egg with a blind side to her.'
Defined the actress in an interview during a filming period that was enjoyed by a happy cast and crew.

With six episodes in all, the series comes to a silly sort of close where the guys manage to get themselves out of a major pickle.

Across each 55 minutes story, the last one proves an eye-opener for Jenny fans. Only glimpsed in the excellent opening credits which provide a swift catch-up of the past-glories of the gang, Jenny's previously-sedate character becomes embroiled in helping the lads escape a siege by acting as a decoy. This is where she returns dressed in red leather zip-up cat suit complctc with thigh-high PVC boots and ridiculous black wig ala The Magic Door. You really have to see it to disbelieve it and watch Mo's proud reaction from within the confines of the pub that they find themselves surrounded by armed police outside.

The Invisibles just about runs out of credibility in this climactic episode but it is all done so well that the viewer can indulge the incredulity as you would probably enjoyed the various scrapes and mishaps experienced by the gang previously. As Jenny offers in a BBC interview, 'I think William Ivory's writing is different and he demands that you go between high drama and comedy. I hope the audience will enjoy that and just go with it.'

Monday Monday (2008) 30 mins
'…It's never just another day at the office.'
DVD cover.
This 7-part comedy-drama aired in July 2009 on ITV 1 in the 9pm slot, with Jenny cast as Jenny Mountfield, the 'office angel' to a struggling supermarket C.E.O, as portrayed by Peter Wight. Appearing, dare I say it, rather matronly; she does not feature greatly in the episodes set at Butterworth's H.Q, a company whose dictum is 'Where quality counts!'
As Wight's PA, Jenny is decked out neatly in familial décor of tightly pulled-back hair, pearls and 2-piece suits (supplemented here by a snazzy

line of cardigans too) alongside a pedigree cast of small-screen stars including Fay Ripley, Neil Stuke and Holly Aird.

For Jenny fans episode 5 proves of special interest in that her character receives a little more screen time with her loyalty to her boss proving strong in a plot involving blackmail.

Monday, Monday has all the usual ingredients of office life: namely politics, internal relationships, oddbods, gossipers and career-climbers in amongst each of its hourly episodes.

Receiving mixed critical appraisal, much merit was awarded to its appealing cast with critiques including the following:

'…entertaining and well-written British comedy series.' [Daily Mirror]

Whilst Harry Venning of The Stage offered, 'nothing if not likeable.'

'…definitely watchable.'
The Guardian.

A DVD of the series was swiftly released soon after the show concluded its run and features a picture of Jenny on its cover.

Pictured opposite: a montage of Jenny as she appears in Monday, Monday.

Midsommer Murders (2009)
After fulfilling character parts so well in many of these made-for-TV shows Jenny added to her CV with a role here in an episode titled 'The Creeper'. Murders had proven to be a very popular drama

series for ITV and by the time of Jenny's appearance as Lady Isobel Cheatham, the show was in its twelfth series. Former Bergerac star John Nettles took the lead role as a weather-beaten D.C.I in this the sixth episode of what was to be his final series. Coincidentally, The Creeper was directed by Renny Rye who had worked on some episodes of Jenny's 1990 Euro-set show TECX. Jenny and Nettles had co-starred in a Shakespearian television production in the past.

jenny at the theatre

At the still tender age of 17 Jenny had acted in I Start Counting, Walkabout and The Railway Children films and turned her energies towards the theatre as a response to a dearth of subsequent cinematic roles. She turned first to Farnham Rep, where her introduction to the theatre business was not a good one: a flop production of restoration comedy School for Scandal. Unfortunately, audiences just did not laugh and often remained silent at key moments when a giggle or snigger was at least expected! By the early-1980s her fortunes had changed dramatically and Jenny was working with the prestigious Royal Shakespeare Company (aka the RSC) following initial exposure at the National Theatre back in the early-1970s. She had wanted to be fully-trained in the art of theatre acting and did a year with the National theatre after being offered a place when she was barely 20. A year later she went off to America and into films as well as some American theatre roles.

The School for Scandal (1970)

Jenny portrayed Lady Teazle in this Farnham Rep production of the comedy of manners from this much-loved Sheridan work. Its slight plot has proved to be a favourite amongst theatre-goers from its inception back in 1777 when rehearsals began on the play even before the playwright had completed the piece. Jenny's character marries into a titled family after coming from a simple country background. She then develops into a scandal monger within those around and about her.
The production was not an enjoyable experience for Jenny as audiences just did not seem to recognize the comedic moments in this Restoration comedy. Farnham Rep was established as a professional company in 1939 and is nowadays known as New Farnham Rep.

Rooted (1970)

Jenny made her London stage debut in this Alexander Buzo play presented at the tiny Hampstead Theatre Club, London. Notable playwrights such as Michael Frayn, Harold Pinter and Hanif Kureishi have all seen early works presented there and I believe Jenny would have performed at the temporary portacabin space at Swiss Cottage, north west London. According to the venues' own website, 'The portacabin became a much-loved performance space by writers, directors, actors and audience alike'. A new, more substantial building opened in 2003.

Arms and the Man (1971)

The author can remember studying this delightful George Bernard Shaw play when it was a part of the syllabus for 'O' Level English Literature back in the 1980s. Jenny stepped into the part of Raina Petkoff, in amongst a cast highlighted by Tom 'Billy Liar' Courtenay and Brian Cox in the Manchester 69 Theatre Company production at The Royal Exchange, Manchester. Formed in the previous year, the company produced some 21 shows over the prevailing 5 years. Man had been on a national tour of the provinces and had previously played to audiences in Sheffield, Nottingham, York and Brighton prior to fulfilling its sold-out, 3-week run in Manchester.

Its opening night took place on 16 May. The Royal Exchange Theatre grew from the confines of the old Cotton Exchange, once boasting as being the largest room for commerce worldwide. Much innovative reconstruction has seen the structure change since Jenny's appearance there and today, a total of 700 seats (rather than the 450 when she appeared there) are now availableto contemporary audiences.

The Ride across Lake Constance (1972)

This peculiar piece, written by Peter Handke saw Jenny play 2 parts: as a black maid and another character introduced later on into the story. Much enjoyed by both critics and London audiences such was its success that the production transferred to the Mayfair Theatre after an initial run at the Hampstead Theatre. It seems that the characters in the play speak dialogue that in no way relates to the story but nonetheless proves entertaining to the audience. Nigel Hawthorne, Jenny's co-star from King of the Wind (1990) also appeared in the cast.

Critical comments:

'An accepting mind is sufficient to provide one with a most delightful evening.'
(Ref: Harold Hobson, Sun.Times, Nov 1973)

Spring Awakening (1972/3)

Jenny was Thea in this Frank Wedekind-created play originally written back in 1891. The German playwright termed his 3-act piece as a 'tragedy of childhood' and it is also known under the title 'The Awakening of Spring'. The story is told primarily through dialogue delivered from youngsters entering that difficult phase of life: puberty. Spring Awakening was presented at the National, with the production directed by Bill Bryden.

Above: the original theatre programme for Arms and the Man.

The Tempest (1974)

'O, woe the day!'

Back in the early-1970s Peter Hall offered Jenny a role in the National Theatre production of this Shakespearian work. Hall had recently succeeded Laurence Olivier to run the National and it was his production. John Gielgud headed a prestigious cast and the actor has since been acknowledged by Jenny as being of great help in fostering her development. She was not then a stage-trained actress and so the project proved a great learning curve. She would stay with the 'National' for a year prior to an initial foray to gain more adult film roles in America. She had only just turned 21.

The lilted tones of Gielgud; described by Michael York as an 'immensely professional actor', encompassed Shakespearian roles as well as Hollywood fare such as the Dudley Moore comedy Arthur (1980). In latter years he also acted in films like The Shooting Party which coincidentally, starred Edward Fox, Jenny's on-screen hubby in September (1996).

The Tempest was written back amidst the plague epidemic in Britain and took some three years to complete by 1611. Jenny played the role of Miranda, and worked hard like the rest of the cast across an eight-week rehearsal period prior to the opening night. Her ill-fated character was defined as being teen-aged and although initially seeming meek mannered she does have moments of articulation betraying her tender age. Miranda is the daughter of Prospero (Gielgud) in what enthusiasts have deemed a romantic comedy. With an uninhabited island setting, the production incorporated quite a substantial cast.

Also involved was Cyril Cusack, whose daughter Niamh subsequently acted in a couple of projects with Jenny; interestingly enough, as her daughter in the telly version of Agatha Christie's 4.50 from Paddington.

Captain Mainwaring from Dad's Army, Arthur Lowe, was also in this work staged at the Old Vic. Playing Stephano, 'a drunken butler', he garnered very good reviews. Some years later he would go on to portray Jenny's troubled father in Sweet William (1980). Lowe, forever remembered by children of a certain age as the voice of the Mr Men, died of a stroke in his theatre dressing room before an engagement in 1982.

Betrayal (1980)

'I thought of you the other day.'

Written by the 2005 Nobel Prize for Literature recipient Harold Pinter and dedicated to his friend, playwright Simon Gray, the original production had opened at the National Theatre in 1978 with Penelope Wilton and Michael Gambon.

Jenny played the role of Emma in a 3-piece work set initially in 1977 and then going backwards through to 1968. The plot details an emotional triangle made up of human insecurities and betrayal and set in a simple yet very effective format. Ms.Agutter was in the American production at the Boston Playhouse theatre. Beginning its commercial life as a cinema, the Playhouse is now called the Stuart Street Playhouse (due to its address).

A film version of Betrayal, not involving Jenny, was released in 1983 with Silas Marner and Freddie as F.R.0.7 co-star Sir Ben Kingsley in a leading role. Pinter, most famous for his play The Caretaker as well as various film screenplay adaptations, died in 2008.

Hedda (1980)

A nervous Jenny, anxious at being back in front of a live audience after a sustained period away, was given the title role in this Charles Marowitz (after Henrik Ibsen) play staged at the renowned Roundhouse venue in north London. She rented a studio flat in Camden Town, beneath the home of Sweet William writer Beryl Bainbridge.

Now a Grade II* listed building of tremendous visual imposition, the Roundhouse began its life in a very different guise: as a steam engine repair shed back in 1846. More well-known as a music venue (think the Doors, the Who and Hendrix), this unique performance space has in recent years been extensively redeveloped and has welcomed the BBC Electric Proms and the Royal Shakespeare Company.

Returning to Jenny's association with the building, Mr Marowitz is a former journalist, writer and director of numerous projects as well as the Marowitz Shakespeare, an anthology of several adaptations of the great bard's works.

The Unified Field (1981)

Does a musical based upon the life of Albert Einstein sound a promising premise? Jenny appeared in just that show at the Mark Taper Forum in Los Angeles, back in 1981. The theatre has a pristine reputation amongst the arts in America and annually receives more than 250k audience figures. Jenny associates Angela Lansbury and Peter Ustinov also appeared there during their own careers.

Arden of Faversham (1982)

This was one of a trio of RSC productions that Jenny featured in back in 1982. Here she played Alice Arden, in amongst a juicy plot set in Elizabethan times and billed as a domestic tragedy involving murder and scandal.

Directed by Terry Hands, this anonymous piece finds Alice's husband murdered by someone requested to do so by his wife (as portrayed by Jenny). It played to audiences at Stratford and London.

King Lear (1982)

Written by William Shakespeare, Jenny was Regan, one of Lear's three daughters, with the title role notably filled by Michael Gambon. Directed by Adrian Noble, who also steered a number of other productions, this Lear is fondly remembered by him for its intensive rehearsal period prior to opening at the RSC in Stratford and then on to London. This was the first such production by them and the play ran for nearly 3 and half hours with an interval breaking it in half.

The Sunday Times was especially complimentary about it and in particularly, Gambon's performance as Lear. James Fenton wrote of Jenny, 'Miss Kestleman (she played Goneril) and Miss Agutter give quite similar and striking portrayals of elegant evil…' Many of the cast members were also doubling-up in the Edward Bond play Lear. Jenny's stage husband, the Duke of Cornwall, was coloured by popular actor Pete Postlethewaite.

Critical comments:

'This is a fine production and an important play.' (Ref: James Fenton, Sunday Times, July 1982)

Lear (1982)

Jenny was given the role of Fontanelle, daughter of Lear (Bob Peck) in this production directed by Barry Kyle which took Shakespeare's King Lear as its starting point. It proved to be playwright Edward Bond's most contentious and popular work of the time. Defining himself as an 'extremist' the London-born scribe's work has fallen out favour somewhat in recent years but this was originally premiered at the Royal Court in 1972 with Harry Andrews in the lead role to great applause. Lear's premise develops into a contemporary tale investigating violence in all its manifestations.

Playwright Mark Ravenhill, a Bond enthusiast, interviewed him for the Guardian newspaper in 2006 and termed the 1971 piece '…an epic rewriting of Shakespeare…the greatest play in the English language exploring what its theme of insanity and power, justice and revenge mean for the modern world.'

The Body (1983)

With a story synopses of an eccentric west country grouping having to deal with the many affects brought on by an American air force base being sited on its doorstep, this Nick Darke piece played at the RSC's Stratford home.

Darke was an actor/ playwright that had seen much of his own work staged by the RSC, the National Theatre and others. The Body ran at the Pit in 1983 and London also.

The Shrew (1984)

Continuing their theatrical association, The Shrew was the second time that Jenny and writer/ director Charles Marowitz worked together in America. Back in 1980 Jenny had played the lead in Hedda, and here she was Kate, in a free adaptation of Shakespeare's The Taming of the Shrew. Marowitz used many scenes from the original tale interspersed with his own contemporary scenes.

Breaking the Silence (1985)

'It has been a lovely play to work on.'

Jenny from a correspondence with a fan.

Written by Glorious 39 writer/ director Stephen Poliakoff, notorious for his incest-ridden 1991 film Close my Eyes, Breaking the Silence was his ninth successful work.

Jenny was cast in the challenging role of Polya, a servant, in the second version of Poliakoff's Russia-set production when it transferred to the Mermaid Theatre, London in May 1985. It had initially been put on by the RSC the previous year at the Pit in the Barbican Centre, London. This particular piece was the first production brought to the Mermaid by them. The RSC was then celebrating its 25th anniversary since being created back in 1960 in Stratford upon Avon. Sadly the Mermaid is no longer a working theatre and nowadays is in use as a venue for prospective corporate events or whatever is required. London-born Poliakoff failed with his attempt to keep the theatre open in 2006, after leasing the building and staging his own productions before monetary concerns concluded the venture. Now 'The Mermaid Conference & Events Centre', the auditorium today seats 600, whilst all the building is available for general hire. Poliakoff would later incorporate television and film projects but was predominantly known for his theatre back then.

Ms.Agutter's role was originally played by Juliet Stevenson and the whole cast of seven changed all apart from Gemma Jones who was retained. Set in 1920, the future Emmy award-winning playwright was inspired to write the story after hearing from his own grandfather of life in the pre-Soviet Union. Jones has since acted in a number of British films and featured alongside Jenny in the 1971 television working of The Cherry Orchard. She also featured recently in post-Jenny series of BBC series Spooks. Breaking the Silence, a romance with much historical and psychological emphasis, was again performed in 2008 (but not involving Jenny).

Critical comments:

'One of the best plays of 1984 and one of the most thrilling individual works of the last decade or two.' (Ref: John Peter, Sunday Times as quoted in the Methuen script of the play, published 1986).

'Jenny Agutter takes over from Juliet Stevenson the role of the maid, and is, like her, left to deal with some of the most difficult passages of an evening that

occasionally lurches into a Soviet rerun of Pygmalion.'
(Ref: Sheridan Morley, Punch, 5 June 1985)
'The tale is exciting, full of fascinating detail, and allows Miss Agutter to be charming…'
(Ref: John Barber, Telegraph, 29 May 1985)

Breaking the Code (1987)

It remains unclear as to whether Jenny was involved in this Hugh Whitemore-created play when it was presented both in Washington D.C and at the Neil Simon Theatre on Broadway.
She did portray a character called Pat Green at the latter venue, a 1445-seater theatre originally known as the Alvin before being re-titled in 1983. The theatre there dates back to the 1930s and has welcomed many names over the prevailing decades including one Gertrude Lawrence. Jenny would portray her screen daughter Pamela in the 1967 film of Gertie's life called Star!
The ever-green Richard Chamberlain, Jenny's co-star in The Man in the Iron Mask (1977) has also appeared at the Anvil complex.

Love's Labour's Lost (1995)

One of the lesser-known Shakespearian plays, Jenny joined the RSC touring production that played in Britain (that year's Edinburgh Festival at the Festival Theatre) and Tokyo, Japan.

RSC
ROYAL SHAKESPEARE COMPANY
Sponsored by ALLIED DOMECQ
EDINBURGH FESTIVAL THEATRE

Tuesday 28 March - Saturday 1st April 1995
EDINBURGH FESTIVAL THEATRE TRUST welcomes the
ROYAL SHAKESPEARE COMPANY

LOVE'S LABOUR'S LOST
by WILLIAM SHAKESPEARE
Directed by IAN JUDGE

She was cast as Rosaline, Princess of France in this production directed by Ian Judge in January of that year. It was running at the Festival from March to April 1995. Jenny also features in the 1985 telly production of the play for the BBC.

Peter Pan (1997)

This particular piece was of great significance to Jenny as when she was taken to the theatre as a child she desparately wanted to fly like those on stage! However, she settled for an acting career instead but did realise such an ambition in a brief scene in Amazon Woman on the Moon (1987).
Just as E.Nesbit's The Railway Children continues to enthral more than a century since its inception, so to does J. M. Barrie's Peter Pan or The Boy Who Would Not Grow Up. As a three-hour show featuring 5 acts, this London production saw Jenny in the role of Mrs Darling. Staged initially at the Royal National Theatre, previews commenced early- December in readiness for its opening night of the 16th.
This latest version, of a play written the same year as The Railway Children, was shaped by Trevor Nunn and director John Caird with Sir Ian McKellen having fun in the dual roles of Captain Hook and Mr Darling.
Not surprisingly, with sterling production values coupled with a classic story and marvellous cast, the production fulfilled a

sell-out run at the National. It transferred to the Oliver stage for some months after.

Critical comments:

'A feast of nursery nostalgia, wizard effects, Edwardian lingo and tinselled adventure.'
(Ref: Observer newspaper)

'On the first night of Peter Pan there was a child who wouldn't grow up inside every one of the audience.'
(Ref: Independent on Sunday)

Rites of Passage (2002)

Jenny appeared with the Polmear Ambache Duo at the John Leggott Hall, Scunthorpe in January 2002. They were then in the midst of a national tour which incorporated music and vocals.

Equus (2007)

'A huge hit all over again.'

Jenny returned to this Peter Schaffer play in 2007 albeit in a different role from the one which she played in the film. She had been the sexually-charged Jill Mason in the 1977 Sydney Lumet film and has since stated that Schaffer was involved in both the film and theatre productions. Now in his early 80s, the playwright worked on minor rewrites for the theatrical revival. For him, Equus was a complicated piece to structure but he had been compelled to pursue it due to an anecdotal incident some years previously.

Appearing in the 2007 run which starred Harry Potter poppet Daniel Radcliffe in the Peter Firth role as Alan, Jenny said it proved an enjoyable time. Radcliffe created Beatlemania-type interest in his involvement in the production with Jenny now cast as Hesther, originally played in the movie by Eileen Atkins.

Staged at the Gielgud Theatre, London prior to a successful Broadway run (but not with Jenny's subsequent involvement) the theatre was renamed as a tribute to the great Shakespearian actor in 1994. However, its origins date back to December 1907 when the venue opened with its seating capacity of 889 on 3 levels. The first play to be performed was actually a musical. Refurbished in 1987, with extensive work on the gold leaf in the auditorium, the theatre is particularly notable for its beautiful circular Regency staircase, oval gallery and tower.

Critical comments:

'Those who saw Equus in the theatre may find the real horses used in the film less majestic and mysterious than the totemic masks of horse heads worn by male actors in the stage version. However, whatever is lost in open-endedness is gained in a vivid sense of equine presence.'
(Ref: F & M A Brussat, from the website spiritualityandpractice.com)

'Jenny Agutter is merely affable as the magistrate; the middle-of-the-road voice of reason.'
(Ref: Kate Bassett, The Independent, 4/3/2007)

'It's a wonderful piece.'

(Author/ performer Steven Fry commenting after attending the opening press night performance). 'The supporting roles are not exactly richly written, but Jenny as a sympathetic magistrate, Jonathan Cullen as Alan's taciturn father, Gabrielle Reidy as his religion-obsessed mother, and Joanna Christie as a sexually exploratory stable girl all do good work.'
(Ref: Michael Billington, Guardian, 28/02/2007)

jenny's audio work

Throughout her long career Jenny has always been admired for her perfect diction and thus has worked consistently in providing voice-over narration for many talking books, documentaries and so forth. The majority of which I detail below but here are some omissions such as 'A Pocket Full of Posies' (2001) a 50 minutes television documentary narrated by Jenny as well as 'World in Art' (2004) a series that she also narrated. However, I feel that the list is as extensive as could be.

1981 - Late Flowering Love, by John Betjeman

Difficult to know where to list this piece: with Jenny giving a voice-over narration only for this interesting project that utilized 4 much-loved works by poet John Betjeman: one of which includes Jenny reading as Joan Hunter in the segment titled 'A Subaltern's Love Song'. Released in July of that year, the music and poems were recorded sometime before the accompanying visuals were added.

1982 - Desert Island Discs

Jenny was interviewed by Roy Plomley for this cult show which allowed guests to select various pieces of favoured music. It went out in May 1982 but the show, created by Plomley, had been running since 1942 and remains popular on its home of Radio 4.

1991 - Rebecca, by Daphne Du Maurier

Jenny and Simon Williams worked together in an audio presentation of this very famous novel. The two would later appear together, as husband and wife, in the BBC TV production A Respectable Trade. That drama coincidentally, co-starred Anna Massey, an actress that also narrated a past version of Rebecca for audio purposes. Single CD or audio cassettes with a running time of 2 hours, 25 mins.

1992 - The Snow Goose, by Paul Gallico

A lovely tale with Jenny providing the narration for a reading presented on BBC radio in December 1992. Comedy madman Spike Milligan had previously provided an interpretation developed from the theme of the work. Jenny also features in a telly documentary called 'The Hollywood Greats', in a programme dedicated to her co-star from The Snow Goose film, Richard Harris. Jenny met Mr Gallico when shooting the television film in the early-1970s (see elsewhere for details).

Taking the Devil's Advice, by Anne Fine
Ultimately known for her children's novels, nonetheless the author also writes adult fiction and this was one such project. A BBC radio play from June 1992.

1993 - Foreign Girls, by Elaine Feinstein
A BBC radio serialisation of a trilogy premiered across November 1993.

The Small Miracle, by Paul Gallico
A lesser-known work from the author of The Snow Goose. Presented by BBC radio in April 1994. The Small Miracle has been made into a film just like The Snow Goose; only it was re-titled Never Take no for an answer.

The Crocodile Bird, by Ruth Rendell
An earlier release in a different format for this one.
(Audio Cassette - 09/ 1993)

1994 - Bad Girls, Good Women, by Rosie Thomas

'Together they broke all the rules...
Penguin audio release.
(Audio Cassette - 07/ 1994)

Thirty Minute Theatre - Love Is Strange, by Peter Thomson
A BBC radio play from April 1993. Actor Malcolm Ward had a role and was also in the Jenny film Sweet William (1980).

1995 - Summer Stories - The Other Girl, by John Mortimer
An adaptation of the late great Mr. Mortimer's work for BBC radio in August 1995.

A Simple Life, by Rosie Thomas
This was Jenny's second project working with the words of Ms.Thomas, a prolific writer of romantic novels.
(Audio Cassette - 06/ 1995)

The Crocodile Bird, by Ruth Rendell
A 1995 audio book recording on the Random House label of a popular novel. Rendell was a former journalist and a successful crime writer.

1996 - Emma: Complete & Unabridged, by Jane Austen
This 1816 tale about the feisty Emma Woodhouse was voiced by Jenny in another excellent feature.
(Audio Cassette - 11/ 1996)

Pride and Prejudice, by Jane Austen
Jenny narrated this work, subsequently released under the 'Classic Fiction' banner.
(Audio CD - 10/ 1996)

The Railway Children, by Edith Nesbit
'Keep off the tracks, Bobbie!'
A lovely voice work of the perennial children's favourite. Dinah Sheridan, Jenny's screen mother from the 1970 film had also provided her lilting tones prior to this interpretation. That particular recording was released on the EMI 'Listen For Pleasure' label in 1977.
(Audio Cassette - 07/ 1996)
Snippets of dialogue lifted from the film soundtrack feature on the official Lionel Jeffries-narrated LP released on the M.F.P label.

Poetry Please by AA Milne
Jenny reads a selection of poetry from the Winnie the Pooh man for this popular BBC Radio 4 show. Presented in June 1996, 2009 marks the 30th anniversary of the show.

The Great Elephant Chase, by Gillian Cross
Ms.Cross is a popular children's author and was the recipient of the 1992 Whitbread Children's novel award.
(Audio Cassette - 06/ 1996)

1997 - With Great Pleasure

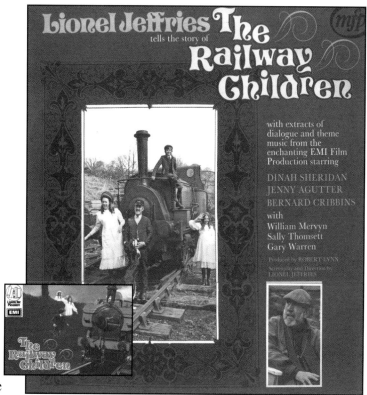

A selection of favoured poetry and prose was selected by Jenny for this long-running, Radio 4 programme. Oddly, the selected works were not read by her but rather by Sara Kestelman and Michael Pennington. The former worked with Jenny on the radio play Embers by Sandor Marai. This 'arts and drama' show aired in November 1997.

Short Story - My Son, by Jane Rawlinson
BBC radio, October 1997.

Lizard Artists

Jenny Agutter interviewed local Cornish artists for this BBC radio programme which aired that July.

An American Werewolf in London, by John Landis/ Dirk Maggs

This audio presentation was made for the BBC Radio Collection and featured Jenny and the wonderful Brian Glover (he was one of the men in the creepy pub). Landis brought in Dirk Maggs to write up and expand upon his own cult classic film from 1981. Produced by Maggs with Jenny reprising her part of Alex Price and John Woodvine also featuring.
(Audio Cassette & CD - 05/ 1997)

The Journals of Dorothy Wordsworth

Read by its adaptor, Sue Rodwell with Jenny also involved. Dorothy was the sister of poet William and was also a writer but had nothing published in her lifetime.
(Audio Cassette - 09/ 1997 / Audio CD - 11/ 2002)

The Tenant of Wildfell Hall: Complete & Unabridged, by Anne Bronte

Jenny was joined by actress Alex Jennings for this project, the only novel from the author. (Audio Cassette - 08/ 1997 / Audio CD - 10/ 2001)

Jamaica Inn, by Daphne Du Maurier

A series of 10 radio episodes were read by Jenny for the BBC across 1996/7. A real page-turner, the novel was originally published in 1936 and made into a film by Alfred Hitchcock three years later.

Pride and Prejudice, by Jane Austen

Another Austen work narrated by Jenny and released on CD by Cambridge Literature. The second CD packaging of the same project.
(Audio CD - 04/ 1997).

1998 - The Feast of Stephen, by Maeve Binchy

A BBC radio production was aired in December '98 of this seasonal short story (published under the collective title 'This year it will be different').

Visiting Royalty, by Sonia Lambert

One of a number of short stories written by the London-based author. Presented in April 1998.

A Respectable Trade, by Philippa Gregory

Jenny narrated this novel from Ms.Gregory and acted in the television adaptation of it too (which was shown on the BBC the same year).
(Audio Cassette - March 1998)

Your Blue-Eyed Boy: Complete & Unabridged, by Helen Dunmore

The first of a couple of Jenny/ Helen Dunmore collaborations, this came under the psychological thriller banner.
(Audio Cassette - 12/ 1998)

1999 - Airs and Graces: Abridged, by Erica James.

Published in 1997 this was the third novel from Erica James which was again on the best sellers list. An Orion Audio Books release was narrated by Jenny across a running time of some 3 hours in this tale of village life.

(Audio Cassette - 01/ 2000)

Bloodline, by Sidney Sheldon

The first of 2 Sheldon projects worked on by Jenny, Bloodline was the fourth novel from the prolific American-born author.

The Other Side of Midnight, also written by Sidney Sheldon

The second novel published by Sheldon after gaining initial success back in 1969 when his first book was released.

Act of Faith: Abridged, by Erica James

Another romantic tale, this time a 1999 work.

(Audio Cassette - 10/ 1999)

Shell Songs, by Clare Boylan

A BBC Radio 4 programme from June 1999 by the Irish-born novelist/ short story writer/ journalist.

A Sense of Belonging: Abridged, by Erica James

Presented after the novel was published in 1998 from the Hampshire-born author.

(Audio Cassette - June 1999)

A Breath of Fresh Air: Abridged, by Erica James

Erica James and Jenny Agutter would prove to be a formidable audio partnership with Jenny recording her lovely narration for a number of novels from the award-winning Ms.James.

This was the first of their many pairings and probably by the time that you are reading this the list would have grown but here is an up-to-date list at the time of writing. A Breath of Fresh Air was published as a novel back in 2000, and tells the story of a 34-year-old woman recently widowed and returning to the village where she grew up.

(Audio Cassette -06/ 1999)

2000 - Dusty Answer: Complete & Unabridged, by Rosamond Lehmann

This was the first novel by a popular British author that was published in 1927.

(Audio Cassette - November 2000)

Zennor in Darkness: Complete & Unabridged, by Helen Dunmore

Jenny narrated this 1993 novel which was released by 'Sterling Edition' on audio cassette in July 2000. Respected author John Le Carre labelled the book as 'a beautiful and inspired novel.'

Heidi, by Joanna Spyri
Released under the DK Read & Listen label, this truly perennial favourite for children across the world saw a new audio version of the tale of the little girl with Jenny as one of the vocal contributors to the project.

Madame Bovary, by Gustave Flaubert
Subsequently adapted into a number of films, Jenny is credited as the reader for this classic work. Madame Bovary is regarded as one of the greatest novels ever and generated enormous notoriety when originally published due to its subject matter.
(Audio Cassette - 06/ 2000)

The White Cat, by Edith Nesbit
Jenny continued her fond association with the author of The Railway Children for this BBC Radio 3 show presented in January 2000.
The White Cat was one of a collection of original stories published in the form of a single book. It tells the tale of a boy who finds a china cat in an attic and soon discovers its powers as a magical talisman.

2001 - Precious Time, by Erica James
Published in 2001, this was a tale of a mum and her young son deciding to head off in a camper van and affecting those that they come into contact with at a local village. Jenny narrates this, the seventh novel from the author.

(Audio Cassette - 25/ 10/ 2001)

The Secret Garden, by Frances Hodgson Burnett
Jenny worked on this 75 minutes 'Junior Classics' (abridged) version of the classic 1911 book subsequently released on CD, it was given away free in a national newspaper.
(Audio Cassette - 11/ 2001)

Music and Silence: Complete & Unabridged, by Rose Tremain
This was the lucky novel number 13 from an author whose first book was published in 1976. Set in the court of Danish King Christian IV, the collected running time of this 14 tape set is a mammoth 18+ hours.
(Audio Cassette - 09/ 2001)

The Jane Austen Collection: Persuasion, Pride and Prejudice, Sense and Sensibility
A smashing cast read these Austen classics and includes the equally sumptuous-sounding Juliet Stevenson, Jenny and Teresa Gallagher.
(Audio Cassette - 09/ 2001)

Ballet Stories, by David Angus
An abridged version was released on the 'Juniour classics' category of this Naxos Audio books from 2001. Stories included were Swan Lake, Giselle, Coppelia, The Nutcracker Suite and Sleeping Beauty. Audio CD - 07/ 2001)

I Capture the Castle: Complete & Unabridged, by Dodie Smith

Read by Jenny, this was the 1948 debut novel by Ms.Smith and was made into a film in 2003.
(Audio Cassette - 04/ 2001 / Audio CD - 12/ 2003)

The Rope and Other Stories: Complete & Unabridged, by Philippa Pearce

The first of two books that Jenny narrated by the late Phillipa Pearce. The format was to feature 8 atmospheric tales collected together.
(Audio Cassette - 03/ 2001)

Bad Blood: A Memoir, by Lorna Sage

This memoir was the winner of the Whitbread Book Price in 2001 but sadly the author had died before receiving the award.
(Audio Cassette - February 2001)

The Holiday, by Erica James

Published in 2000, the novel tells the tale of a youngish-woman's travel holiday in Corfu.
(Audio Cassette - 01/ 2001)

2002 - Flames - Monday Lunch in Fairyland, by Angela Huth

Premiered on BBC Radio in October 2002, Flames was one of nearly a dozen works in the CV of Ms.Huth.

Opposite: DVD cover of documentary Marine Team.

Hidden Talents, by Erica James

The plot of this 2002 novel centered around a group attending a creative writing class. Jenny recorded a set of 4 audio tapes with a running time of 6 hours.
(Audio Cassette - 09/ 2002)

A Dog So Small: Complete & Unabridged, by Philippa Pearce

A paperback 'Read Along' featuring Jenny was released in September 2002. The book was published back in 1962 with the author understanding her young audience perfectly. The Guardian termed her 'one of the finest children's writers of her generation.' She died in 2006.

2003 - Marine Team: Rescue, Rehabilitation & Release

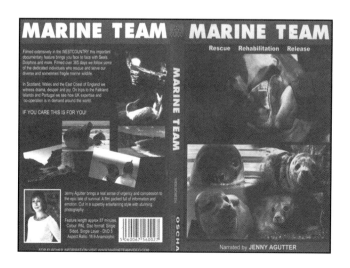

Jenny provided the narration-only across its 87 minutes running time. The film follows a year in the lives of various bands of dedicated agencies and individuals rescuing injured wild life across the world. Its back cover blurb includes a portrait photograph of Jenny and states, 'Jenny brings a real sense of urgency and compassion to the epic tale of survival. A film packed full of information and emotion.' And continues, 'Cut in a superbly entertaining style with stunning photography.' Marine Team was made and released by Oscha productions and if you would like to support the organisations featured therein, please contact either of these two websites: www.bdmlr.org.uk marineteamvideo.com

2004 - Love and Devotion, by Erica James

Published in 2005 this one follows characters Harriet Swift and Will Hart through their various trials and tribulations.
(Audio Cassette - 10/ 2004)

Private Passions

Presenter Michael Berkeley invited Jenny to talk about her musical likes and dislikes and how they affected her life. This BBC Radio 3 show aired in September 2004 with Jenny choosing pieces from popular composers such as Brahms, Elgar and Shostakovich.

Time for a Change: Abridged, by Erica James

With a running time of a little over 6 hours, Jenny narrated this story in a 4 cassette audio release. The first in a long line of novels by the author.

Emma Brown: Complete & Unabridged, by Clare Boylan

A novel fashioned from some dozen pages of an original manuscript following the death of author Charlotte Bronte. An abridged, 6 hours version was released on the Orion label.
(Audio Cassette - 05/ 2004 / Audio CD - 06/ 2004)

Embers, by Sandor Marai

This 90 minute tale aired on Radio 3 with Jenny as Krisztina in an adaptation by Lou Stein of a best-selling novel by the Hungarian author who committed suicide in 1989. A stellar cast was headlined by X Men star Patrick Stewart as her fictional husband. The tale tells the revenge being sought by an elderly man (Stewart) against a man that once had an affair with his young wife (as portrayed by Jenny).

Paradise House, by Erica James

Jenny provided the narration for this 4 audio cassette release described by Our Time magazine in 2004 as 'Erica James at her best...a wonderful read.'
(Audio Cassette - October 2003 / audio CD - 2004)

2005 - Northanger Abbey, by Jane Austen
A BBC offering of a posthumously-published novel detailing the events concerning a visit to Bath. Serialised for radio in three parts in 09/ 2005.

The Amazing Story of Adolphus Tips: Complete & Unabridged, by Michael Morpurgo
Jenny joined the author in providing vocal talents for this popular children's author tale set in World War II.
(Audio Cassette - 04/ 2005)

My Love Must Wait, by Nick Warburton
Premiered as a BBC radio play in January 2005, the talented Warburton has written children's books, radio, stage, and television scripts. The story was about the life of explore Matthew Flinders: the first man to circumnavigate Australia.

2007 - The Thirteenth Tale, by Diane Setterfield
The Independent newspaper called this best-seller 'a rich multi-layered mystery that twists and turns and weaves quite a magical spell.' Written in the Gothic style, this was her first novel and instantly made her a millionaire. This unabridged version was read by Ms.Agutter.
(Audio CD - 06/ 2007).

The Best of Elizabeth Gaskell
Read by actress Maggie Ollerenshaw and Jenny, Ms.Agutter reads 'North and South,' a Victorian period drama by an author known as 'Mrs Gaskell'. It is now on the Further Education college syllabus as a read text. Gaskell wrote an original biography of her friend Charlotte Bronte of whom Jenny has also been associated with.
(Audio CD - 06/ 2007).

2008 - The Rain Before It Falls, by Jonathan Coe
This BBC audio book was an adaptation of the Birmingham-born author's 2007 novel. Coe was termed by fellow writer Nick Hornby as 'the best British novelist of his generation.'
(Audio Cassette/ CD- published 06/ 2008)

Doctor Who: The Bride of Peladon, by Barnaby Edwards
'Classic Doctors - brand new adventures.'
A 4-part story in which Jenny played a supporting character credited as Sekhmet for this adventure with Peter Davison in the guise of the Doctor. Big Finish Productions produced this new recording that came available for sale in January 2008. The story found the doctor re-visiting a planet previously visited by a past incumbent from the 1970s, one Jon Pertwee.
(Audio CD, 01/ 2008 and as as audio download).

Top Cat, White Tie & Tails
Sub-titled 'Guide Dogs for the Blind, volume 3', Jenny reads 2 pieces of work (alongside others) written by folk man Les Barker. The CD was devised as a fund-raising project for the British Computer Association of the Blind.

Miscellaneous:
Wuthering Heights, by Emily Bronte
Jenny narrated this classic tale which was released on The Times audio Library label (Audio Cassette - Date of release unknown).

JENNY AGUTTER

SNAP

OBSERVATIONS OF
LOS ANGELES AND LONDON

references &
websites

Jenny Agutter - Snap: Observations of Los Angeles and London. Quartet books, 1983.

As with most research, I have looked at many sources both printed and web-based, as well as via associates and correspondence. The following is a list of primary sources.

Leslie Halliwell, Film Guide, 6th ed, Paladin, 1987.
Steven H.Scheuer, Movies on TV, 1989-90, Bantam.
Jenny interview: BBC Breakfast, May 2008.
British Television: An Illustrated Guide, compiled for the BFI by Tise Vahimagi,
Oxford University Press, BFI, 1994.
Radio Times Guide to Films 2007, 2006, BBC.
Julie Andrews, An intimate biography, Richard Stirling, Portrait, 2007
James Herbert: Devil in the Dark, Craig Cabell, Metro, 2004.
Stephanie Pinter, Nice to see you! The Bruce Forsyth Story, Northern & Shell, 2008.
The Animated Movie Guide: The Ultimate Illustrated Reference to Cartoon, Stop-motion, and Computer-generated Feature Films
Jerry Beck, Chicago Review Press, 2005
Rogert Ebert's Movie Home Companion 1990 edition, Andrews & McMeel, 1990.
The Futura Illustrated Film Guide, by the editors of Consumer Guide & Jay A.Brown, 1985.
The Guardian, 22 February 2002, Gareth McLean interview with Jenny.
The Penguin TV Companion, 3rd edition, Jeff Evans, Penguin 2006.

Hello Darlin', Larry Hagman,
Simon & Schuster, 2001
Acting My Life: The Autobiography,
Ian Holm, Bantam, 2004.
Blow-up & other exaggerations,
David Hemmings, Robson Books, 2004.
Travelling Player: An Autobiography,
Michael York, Headline, 1991.
Mark Ravenhill interview with Edward Bond,
Guardian, 9 September 2006.
Variety Movie Guide 1999, ed. Derek Elley,
Boxtree, 1999.
The Boxtree Encyclopaedia of TV Detectives,
Geoff Tibballs, Boxtree, 1992.
The Guardian, 22 February 2002: Jenny
interviewed by Gareth Mclean.
Boleslaw Michalek, The Cinema of Andrzej
Wajda, The Tantivy Press, Lon-New York, 1973.
1000 Best movies on Video. Classics for TV,
Peter Waymark, Guild, 1984.

I have scanned many, many sites and have found numerous snippets of information. Much of which has proved useful was located from:

jennyagutter.net
CrazyAboutTV.com
Itv.co.uk
Imdb.co.uk
reddwarf.co.uk
edithnesbit.co.uk
news.bbc.co.uk

www.williamfnolan.com
Agathachrisitie.com
Suspense-movies.com
memorabletv.com
haworth-village.org.uk
www.litarena.com
Marjorie Jones - citizencaine.org
www.guardian.co.uk
http://rogerebert.suntimes.com, rogerebert.com
Roger Ebert, Walkabout review, 1 Jan 1971.
www.wajda.pl - Andrzej Wajda website, director
of Gates of Paradise
www.televisionheaven.co.uk
www.hampsteadtheatre.com
Logan's Run fansites: www.snowcrest.net /
simonmaccorkindale.net or shelliwood.com
The Invisibles: cast interviews from www.bbc.co.uk
The Railway Children-related sites:
www.bluebell-railway.co.uk
www.kwvr.co.uk
For information relating to the 2000 telly version:
http://freespace.virgin.net/peter.culley/thriller.htm

Thanks to:
Tina at the Cystic Fibrosis Trust for the front cover photo (and some inner pics) of Jenny.
If you would like to support any of the number of Jenny associated charities, such as the CFT, you might like to look at the following pages.

jenny's supported charities

hallforcornwall.co.uk
boxoffice@hallforcornwall.org.uk
Back Quay,
Truro, Cornwall
TR1 2LL
01872 321 973

Edith Nesbit Society
edithnesbit.co.uk

Campaign for
Better Transport
bettertranspport.org.uk
info@bettertranspport.org.uk
12-18 Hoxton street,
London N1 6NG
020 7613 0742

jenny's supported charities

The Ovarian Cancer Support Network

ovacome.org.uk

ovacome@ovacome.org.uk

PO Box 6294, London W1A 7WJ

0207 299 6654

Action for Children

care@actionforchildren.org.uk

actionforchildren.org.uk

85 Highbury Park , London

0300 123 2112

RSA: Removing barriers to social progress

thersa.org

general@rsa.org.uk

8 John Adam street,

London WC2N 6EZ

020 7930 5155

Cystic Fibrosis Trust

cftrust.org.uk

enquiries@cftrust.org.uk

11 London road, Bromley, Kent BR1 1BY

0845 859 1000

jenny's supported charities